ALSO BY GEORGE M. JOHNSON

All Boys Aren't Blue

FLAMBOYANTS

THE QUEER HARLEM RENAISSANCE I WISH I'D KNOWN

GEORGE M. JOHNSON

ILLUSTRATED BY **CHARLY PALMER**

FARRAR STRAUS GIROUX · NEW YORK

*To the people who choose to live in their unapologetic truths,
despite a world that continues to try to dim their light. —G. M. J.*

Farrar Straus Giroux Books for Young Readers
An imprint of Macmillan Publishing Group, LLC
120 Broadway, New York, NY 10271 • mackids.com

Our books may be purchased in bulk for promotional, educational, or
business use. Please contact your local bookseller or the Macmillan
Corporate and Premium Sales Department at (800) 221-7945, ext. 5442,
or by email at MacmillanSpecialMarkets@macmillan.com.

Library of Congress Cataloging-in-Publication Data is available.

First edition, 2024
Book design by Samira Iravani
Printed in China

ISBN 978-0-374-39124-9
1 3 5 7 9 10 8 6 4 2

CONTENTS

INTRODUCTION   1

"SECRET NOT SECRET"   7

LANGSTON HUGHES   11

COUNTEE CULLEN   21

JOSEPHINE BAKER   31

"IN THIS ESSAY . . ."   39

RICHARD BRUCE NUGENT   43

MA RAINEY   53

ALAIN LOCKE   63

BESSIE SMITH   73

"WE GET LIT"   81

GLADYS BENTLEY   85

CLAUDE MCKAY   93

JIMMIE DANIELS   101

"CAN YOU ANSWER ME THIS?"   107

ETHEL WATERS   111

ZORA NEALE HURSTON   119

"FLAMBOYANTS"   127

RECOMMENDED READING   129

FLAMBOYANT *ADJ.*

/flæmˈbɔɪənt/

(of people or their behavior) different, confident, and exciting in a
way that attracts attention

brightly colored and noticeable

— *Oxford Learner's Dictionaries*

QUEER *N.*

/ˈkwir/

a : a person who is gay, lesbian, bisexual, pansexual, or otherwise
not heterosexual

b : a person whose gender identity is nonbinary or differs from the
sex they had or were identified as having at birth : a genderqueer
or transgender person : a person who is not cisgender

Usage of Queer

While the noun *queer* is used as a neutral or positive self-descriptor,
it has a long history of pejorative use and is likely to be considered
offensive when used by someone who does not identify as queer.

HARLEM *N.*

/ˈhär-ləm /

2 section of New York City in northern Manhattan bordering on the Harlem and East rivers; a center of African American culture especially in the 1920s

RENAISSANCE *N.*

/ˈre-nə-ˌsän(t)s/

2 . . . a movement or period of vigorous artistic and intellectual activity

3 : REBIRTH, REVIVAL

—Merriam-Webster

HARLEM RENAISSANCE *N.*

1. a renewal and flourishing of Black literary and musical culture during the years after World War I in the Harlem section of New York City.

—Dictionary.com

OUT OF DARKNESS

You can ban our books, but you can't ban our story
Berate us and chide us,
The fear is behind us,
The light bestowed upon us is from a spirit higher than human
You won't ban guns, but you'll ban the books,
America, land of the free, home of the crook,
Why does our sexuality have you shook?
The light bestowed upon us is from a spirit higher than human
This land is bought and paid for by kin,
Land of the slave, the indigenous tribes,
You can tell the lies, but we see it with our eyes,
The light bestowed upon us is from a spirit higher than human
You can no longer tell the alternative version,
Black, Queer, we been here, we have proof,
Cemented are their names, in concrete is their truth,
The light bestowed upon us is from a spirit higher than human
Those who lived in the shadows, now live in the light
Mighty is our plight,
It won't stop our fight,
As the children of the ancestors our truths are taking flight
The words of this book become the fist with all the might
And even if you ban this, the bark ain't as strong as our bite
Our stories are finally in the light
Are the light
The light

INTRODUCTION

M Y HEROES WERE HIDDEN FROM ME.
In school, I was forced to learn about this country's "forefathers." You know, the famous guys who came before us and supposedly built this country. There was George Washington, known as the most popular general of the American Revolution and first president of the United States. And there was Abraham Lincoln, famously known for "freeing the slaves" with the Emancipation Proclamation. The list goes on: Ben Franklin, Alexander Hamilton, and don't even get me started on Thomas Jefferson.

As a kid, I saw Abraham Lincoln as a hero, my savior for ending American slavery, which ultimately allowed me to be in school alongside my white classmates 130 years later. But those lessons about the forefathers were just an indoctrination process. Textbooks, teachers, curriculums wanted us to think that our history was shaped only by white, heterosexual men who should be viewed (specifically by nonwhite kids) as our saviors. It wasn't.

Despite seeing so few stories about people like me in our history, I still loved to learn and loved to read. So I soaked in all that I could at school, and at times I used the library to find knowledge that I couldn't get in class or at home. My yearning to learn about my own Blackness was often unrelenting. Even back then, I think I knew that my ancestors were going to be part of my salvation and my purpose in adult life.

Which is likely why I was always *so* excited whenever Black History Month rolled around. That glorious month allowed me to immerse myself in my culture and learn the stories of people who shared my skin color. These were the stories of people who were alive alongside my grandparents and great-grandparents. These histories connected my present to the past. Black History Month introduced me to heroes I could easily connect to. Or did it?

Of course, we always talked about Martin Luther King Jr., Malcolm X, Frederick Douglass, Harriet Tubman, and other pillars of Black history. But there were also times—though not as often— when we got to learn about less famous heroes like Josephine Baker, Lorraine Hansberry, Langston Hughes, and James Baldwin. Perhaps that's because there is something very different about the first four people versus the later four. A difference that could have made all the difference to me: being Black *and* queer.

I often say that it is hard for someone to look in the mirror and see a reflection when they can't see any reflections of themselves out in the world. That was my experience growing up. By the age of five, I knew I was different from all the other little boys in my class. My flamboyant mannerisms and my point of view just weren't in line with the way society wants boys to act, talk, and dress. And with little access to the stories of Black queer people who came before me, I felt alone and unseen.

As a Black queer child, I had the right to know that Black queer people existed before me. I had the right to know that the things I was feeling and experiencing had been felt and lived by millions of others. They paved the road for me to walk on. Yet that road was hidden from me and so many others, obscured by a society that deemed any identity outside of heterosexuality to be nefarious. As a result, I felt unacceptable in society.

And society is still trying to block, hide, and steal our Black and queer stories. My debut young-adult memoir, *All Boys Aren't Blue*, is currently one of the most banned and challenged books in the United States. It has been removed from library shelves in many school districts. It is not by chance but by design that Black queer stories are still being attacked and hidden away today.

Only in my late teens and well into my adulthood did I come to find out the truth about many of the people profiled in this book. And as I continue to look into the past, I'm discovering more and more people who were Black queer pioneers in a myriad of ways. Black queer people have always permeated every facet of life. Even when they were "closeted"—that is, even when they didn't publicly share their full identity—they made a cultural impact during their lifetime that continues to be felt.

So many people try to say that queerness is some new phenomenon. The reality, however, is that queerness is as old as heterosexuality. And Blackness is inherently queer. You can't have one that isn't inclusive of the other. I like to operate under the Ghanaian principle of *sankofa*, which translates to "to go back and get it." It's a process of reaching back to knowledge gained in the past and bringing it into the present in order to make positive progress. That is what this book is. We can't make positive progress as Black queer folks if we don't tell the stories of Black queer folks before us—especially if those stories have been suppressed or told inaccurately.

I chose to write about the Harlem Renaissance because it has always been seen as one of the queerest historical periods. The Harlem Renaissance was a time when the Black community took great risks in the arts. Many icons of the Harlem Renaissance became worldwide phenoms, even if they never fully received their flowers here in the United States. Others, though, never got to see their names in bright lights or on book covers, despite changing the world for so many of us. This book celebrates their differences with the excitement and attention they have always deserved.

May the flamboyant Black and queer ancestors of the past be remembered for the light they shone during a time that forced them to live in the dark. Our Black and queer icons of the past should be hidden no more.

SECRET NOT SECRET

Dear Reader of this letter,
Whoever you are

I've got a secret that nobody knows
Exceptin' me, them, and some other folk
To the world, I live (in a box) for fame
In the dark and shadows, I am the flame

Maybe I'll tell my secret aloud
Or maybe the secret will tell on me, child,
Known or unknown, we all are grown
Doing grown-people things, you know   what I'm sayin',

Will they accept me if my secret is found
Or will they bury my truth with me in the ground
Only time will tell, or will I—
The secret of "sin," a public life of lies

Whoever you are,
Dear Reader of this letter

Can you keep my secret?

LANGSTON HUGHES

BORN: FEBRUARY 1, 1901, JOPLIN, MISSOURI
DIED: MAY 22, 1967, NEW YORK CITY, NEW YORK
POET, PLAYWRIGHT, ACTIVIST, NOVELIST

I LOVE WRITING. I think I always knew that I would be a writer, or at minimum would one day have a story to tell. Writing is one of those things that can come in many different forms. Poems, music, essays, letters—each has a special ability to convey my feelings and opinions. When I think about Langston Hughes, a person who wrote in many different forms and styles, I think about what inspired me to uphold his legacy with this book. A book that honors him and other Black queer creatives from one of the most pivotal times in history.

Even with the minimal information I got at school during Black History Month, certain figures have always stayed in my memory bank. Langston was one of those figures, because I always felt connected to his poetry. It felt poignant but secretive at the same time. There was a softness and vulnerability to his writing, which always made me wonder if there was more to his story. More to the lens through which he saw the world. Maybe in looking at him, I wondered if he and I saw the world through the same set of lenses—Black and queer.

But before we get into it, I think it's important to address some scrutiny around Langston's identity. There has been much debate about his sexuality. Most scholars believe that he was, in fact, queer.

Although no partner, man or woman, has ever been linked to him, his writing often alluded to homosexuality and some of his experiences within it. Many of his friends, who were also prominent folks of that time, were indeed queer.

Langston's life speaks evidently to the history of Black queerness. I know what it feels like to be a closeted queer person, or non-public about my sexuality and identity. Being closeted often meant sacrificing my true happiness in order to survive and stay safe. Until I was about twenty-seven years old, I didn't publicly identify as gay. I finally did so in an article I wrote.

James Mercer Langston Hughes was born in 1901 to James Hughes and Caroline Mercer Langston—hence his name, which he shortened to just Langston Hughes. After separating from his mother, his father moved to Mexico, stating he was tired of the racism he faced in America. Langston's mother would often leave him for long periods in order to work, so he was primarily raised by his grandmother, Mary Patterson Langston.

It's interesting how relatable this piece of his story is for me and many others. Although I had both parents at home, my parents worked a lot, too. So my grandmother, whom I called Nanny, was my main caregiver for many years. And just like Nanny, I love how it is said that Langston's grandmother instilled in him the power of oral traditions—the passing down of history, art, culture, and storytelling from generation to generation through vocal communication. She also taught him how important it is to help your community, take pride in being Black, and always support those who have less than you. In reading about Langston's life, I felt like a damn mirror was being held up to my face and my own experiences. I was taught the same values he was taught.

A rift developed between Langston and his father after his father left the United States. However, Langston found his love of writing during this time. He began writing poetry in junior high and high school. It is said that while he attended Central High School in Cleveland, Ohio, his teacher Helen Maria Chesnutt pushed him to be a writer. He wrote for his high school paper, and even began writing plays and poetry.

When it came time for Langston to go to college, he was met with an ultimatum. James Hughes was a lawyer and believed that Langston should go to school for engineering, despite his gifts as a writer. He agreed to pay for college, but only if Langston studied engineering.

I can relate to this, as I think many teenagers can. My father wasn't as bad as Langston's. For starters, he was around and showed his love for me in many ways. But he *did* want me to go to a local community college instead of leaving town. Sometimes parents think they know what is best; many times they do, but not always. Despite my father's wishes, I got my way. And so did Langston—sort of. He agreed to study engineering, but only if he could go to Columbia University.

Langston started his engineering studies at Columbia in 1921, but he continued writing under a pen name. The following year, he left school due to the immense racism he was receiving from classmates. He was also not allowed to live on campus. After he left Columbia, he found solace in the nearby neighborhood of Harlem, where he felt at home within its Blackness and culture.

Although the Harlem Renaissance is seen as one of the queerest periods in Black History, especially in the United States, it doesn't mean that said queerness was accepted. I think *grudging tolerance* better describes what queer people experienced during that time. I can only imagine that Langston, who became a leader in the Harlem

Renaissance, never felt the space or security to be publicly queer. There were reasons—both internal and external—informing his decision to obscure his sexuality.

Despite this, he carved a pathway for Black thought, ideas, and creativity. Langston was a college professor, mentor, activist, bestselling poetry writer, playwright, and cultural thought leader. One of my favorite poems by him is "Let America Be America Again." It is an amazing dual-point-of-view poem about the founding ideology of America versus the reality of the American experience for several groups of people. It's an especially interesting poem for our era because of its contrasting ideas to former president Donald Trump's campaign slogan, "Make America Great Again." The question is, Great for *whom*?

You see, America has been great for neither Black folks, nor queer folks (and not always great for immigrants, especially non-white ones), and has fooled impoverished whites into thinking people of other races or ethnic origins are their enemies. So when I hear the slogan "Make America Great Again," I have to ask what period of American history it is referencing. The period where land was taken from Indigenous people? The periods of slavery and Jim Crow? Our time of extreme anti-LGBTQIA+ bias and hatred?

And here we have Langston Hughes, criticizing these very notions way back in 1936 for *Esquire* magazine, where the poem was published during the Great Depression. But that's who he was. Poignant and honest. And I could sit here and probably write a whole book analyzing his work, but this book is about introducing him to you with the hope that you will go out and learn more about him and others of his time. I hope he will inspire you to write more. Speak more. Do more.

Throughout history, people have fought against the truth, trying to hide it or erase it from history. Some people have tried to deny and rewrite the history of slavery in the United States. Others are Holocaust deniers, who, from the moment it happened to this very day, have tried to lie about what the Nazis did.

These lies are self-serving and hurt us all. The rewriting of our history denies our humanity. It severs our links to the past and allows people in power to deny how those events play a role in every system of oppression we face today. It's why we must remain vigilant in telling the truth and, even more so, correcting the lies of the past in an effort to change our futures.

My favorite piece that Langston ever wrote is an essay titled "Spectacles in Color" from his first autobiography, *The Big Sea*. I was an adult when I first read the essay. It discussed a ball he attended during the 1920s "where the men dress[ed] as women and the women dress[ed] as men." He noted how people paid money to come and watch the "spectacle"—that it was more celebrated as a part of culture than shunned.

This blew my mind. I was introduced to Ballroom culture around 2006, through a college friend. We would go to watch the "Houses"— family-style groups with "mothers," "fathers," and "kids." The Houses are typically named after iconic fashion houses, like Gucci or Balenciaga. But it wasn't until 2014 that I became more involved with Ballroom, helping to put on balls, befriending many in the community, and pitching in with their advocacy efforts. And now I am a member of the House of Comme des Garçons.

I watched the documentary *Paris Is Burning*, which covers many of the House leaders of the late 1980s and early '90s. In 2018, the award-winning show *Pose* debuted, giving us an even deeper look into the world of Ballroom in New York City during that same period. A few years later, the show *Legendary* aired, which depicts what the current Ballroom competitions look like. And the award-winning documentary *KiKi* highlighted a growing part of the Ballroom scene in the 2000s until today.

So when I learned that Ballroom dated back to the late 1800s, I was inspired to carry the baton, to tell readers more about our legacy and culture. There is something beautiful about Langston Hughes capturing a firsthand experience of Black queerness and making sure it was recorded. Specifically, because of him, we know more about our truth.

And that's the saddest part about our history whether it be Black history, queer history, or Black queer history. Approximately ten million Black people were enslaved in this country, yet we have fewer than six thousand recorded accounts of their lives. I often wonder how many of those accounts were from a Black queer perspective. We know only the stories we know. We know some stories only because people like Langston spoke up about the truth in the face of criticism. This is the same work that Black storytellers are doing today. This is why our books continue to be banned. Truth-telling has never been safe for us. But it has always been necessary.

When I wrote my debut memoir, *All Boys Aren't Blue*, I had the ability to write my truth with the full color and texture that many of my ancestors and heroes were denied. I documented my Blackness and my queerness and their intersection in my own words. I think of *Flamboyants* as an expansion not only of Langston's essay "Spectacles in Color" but also of his entire life's work. And one day, someone else's work will be the expansion of mine. To me, that is spiritual and ancestral work. Living through one another's time.

That's how oral and written traditions operate. They've been one of our greatest tools for liberation.

Whenever I need affirmation, I return to "Dreams," one of Langston's most quoted poems.

It speaks so perfectly about life in the imaginative. For me, imagination is where Black freedom resides. In the space of our imagination, we get to create worlds for ourselves outside our oppression. We get to play out our dreams before manifesting them in the real world. Dreams keep us alive.

Langston was a true dreamer. It's reflected throughout all of his work. His poems and essays on love and queerness showcase what the world could be without societal constraints. His criticisms of the time he lived in were a challenge to the oppressor. And his contributions to the arts inspire us to use our words, create our own dreams, and build an America where one day we can all live freely.

COUNTEE CULLEN

BORN: MAY 30, 1903, BALTIMORE, MARYLAND
DIED: JANUARY 9, 1946, NEW YORK CITY
WRITER FOR CHILDREN, POET, NOVELIST, PLAYWRIGHT

"**M**Y GOD TODAY,**"** as the kids would say. Countee Cullen most certainly lived an interesting life. Where to begin? I could start with how I fell in love with his poetic style. Or even how the interconnectedness of Black culture would eventually lead Countee to becoming a teacher for a young James Baldwin, another Black queer icon in his own right. Or I could start with the one story that continues to gag us all. Did you really marry that woman knowing you were a gay man in front of folks who also knew your business?

I'll start with the basics. Countee (who pronounced his name as Coun-tay) had many talents, including being a poet, novelist, and playwright. He was one of the most well-known writers during the Harlem Renaissance. Folks who knew him personally said he was extremely intelligent, having graduated from New York University and been selected as one of eleven members for Phi Beta Kappa, the oldest honor society in the United States. He went on to receive a master's degree from Harvard University. All these accomplishments made him an example of "Black excellence," a concept that will come into play later.

His work was part of the Negritude movement, which focused on discovering Black values and raising Black people's awareness of their place in society—and which was a driving force for many writers during the Harlem Renaissance. In reading his work, I found it interesting how he believed race relations between whites and Blacks needed to improve but placed some of that burden on Black folks—as if to say our assimilation into American identity was as important or more important than owning our Negro identity. I don't believe the oppressed are responsible for fixing relations with their oppressor. We are not the creators of racism, nor do we have power within racist structures. We shouldn't be expected to extend an olive branch to fix it.

That said, I do love his most well-known work, "The Ballad of the Brown Girl." It won him several awards and deservedly so. In the fifty stanzas of the poem, he painted an entire movie. I can see why W. E. B. Du Bois loved his writing, too. It spoke to an elite space that some Blacks occupied. It was opulent and jubilant. However, folks like Langston Hughes had very real concerns about affluent Black leaders like Countee Cullen and W. E. B. Du Bois focusing their art only on the opulence of Blackness, and pushing others to do the same. Langston was like me in wanting Black art to be encompassing of the entire Black experience—the good, bad, and in between.

Part of that *in between* was Countee's sexuality. Outside of literary debates, he was dealing with his own identity crisis. And because Countee was part of the Black elites of his day, he had to process questions about his sexuality while also being a leader in a heteronormative society.

Fortunately for him, friendship and support were found in one of the greatest Black philosophers of that time, Alain Locke. I talk more about him later in this book, but that's the beauty of the Harlem Renaissance: how connected everyone was during that period.

It is said that Alain was like a mentor to Countee, helping him recognize who he truly was early in life. He supported Countee through the process of accepting his love for men. This isn't to say that Countee didn't also have a love for women—only that the societal pressure of heterosexuality and his love of women didn't negate his feelings toward men. The juxtaposition of Black excellence against his identity influenced him throughout his life.

Okay, let's talk about this wedding. Countee was definitely not the first man to marry a woman while still figuring out his sexuality. But to do it in front of three thousand people? He was bold for that one.

Countee's wedding to Yolande Du Bois, W. E. B. Du Bois's daughter, was the talk of the town in Black America. Two things I find most interesting about this whole circus: One, that Countee and W.E.B. planned the wedding with very little input from Yolande. And two, that Countee wasn't known for being flashy. Instead he was quite shy. And yet he agreed to this widely publicized event.

Thankfully, they didn't have social media during those times, because I can only imagine the frenzy that would have ensued— especially following the wedding. I'm sure both parties would have preferred to avoid being the center of attention, with everyone living vicariously through them. But this pairing was built on the notion of Black excellence rather than Black love.

W.E.B. had a theory called "The Talented Tenth." This concept emphasized "the necessity for higher education to develop the leadership capacity among the most able 10 percent of black Americans." He worried that Blacks would be ranked second-class citizens since industrial jobs—the ones Blacks most often held—weren't looked as highly upon as educated professions like teachers, lawyers, or doctors. His philosophy had a limit, though: It excluded women as leaders, as he and many others felt that men were the most inspiring figures within the Black community. Maybe that's the reason he wouldn't even let his daughter plan her own wedding. W.E.B. held tight to the notion of male superiority in addition to class superiority.

Before she married Countee, Yolande was actually in love with a saxophonist she was dating named Jimmie Lunceford. W.E.B. disapproved of him because he was a musician. In a letter to his daughter, W.E.B. stated, "Nothing is more disheartening and idiotic than to see two human beings without cultivated tastes, without trained abilities, and without power to earn a living, locking themselves together and trying to live on love."

Although Countee was struggling with his sexuality at the time, he agreed to marry Yolande. And W.E.B. got to host his "talented tenth wedding." Now, just to note, Countee never chose an identity. In his lifetime, he had relationships with women as well as men. And maybe he never even knew the truth about himself. Rumor has it that Langston Hughes—who knew about Countee's sexuality—not only attended the wedding but also gave the couple a fruit bowl as a gift. Whew—the shade of it all!

I think that wedding was more about the perception of Black excellence than about the truth of Black excellence. It's not wealth, it's not degrees, it's not celebrity. Black excellence is our people making it this far despite a world intent on our death, built on our labor, and profiting off our struggle.

It's said that several months after the wedding, while overseas, Countee finally told Yolande the truth about who he was, admitting his attraction to men.

I can't even imagine the fear that went into him telling his truth. After taking those "sacred" vows in front of so many and being headline news throughout Black America, to know it was built on a huge lie must have been an incredible burden. Yolande immediately told her father she was going to file for a divorce. I gagged when I learned that W.E.B. did the unthinkable and wrote Countee a letter arguing that his daughter's "lack of sexual experience" was the reason why the marriage wasn't working.

Several things to parse out here. First, when a man confesses that he is in love with someone of the same gender, people often blame a woman. I've heard folks say that queer kids tend to come from single-mother homes because there's no man around. Or that gay men can be turned heterosexual with "the right woman." Such flawed logic is an attempt to deny the truth. Queer people know who they are and what they feel.

W. E. B. Du Bois's remarks also speak to how poorly considered women were at that time. He blamed his own daughter for the demise of her marriage. Homophobia is a by-product of misogyny. Queerness in men is seen as an effeminate trait—too close to womanhood—and is thus hated. From my perspective, it is interesting to see W. E. B. Du Bois's misogynistic thoughts being used in this case as a reason for why men might be gay.

Countee and Yolande divorced in 1930, having been married only two years. After this, Countee's work shifted from being race-based to more romantically focused. I often think about the many ways Black artistry becomes a form of escapism. It was one of the many criticisms that the eighteenth-century poet Phillis Wheatley received. Critics felt she should have focused on her existence rather than optimism, love, and many other subjects her work covered. But I think that's the beauty in our art: creating realities outside of our daily lives.

It's very cool that Countee taught English at a junior high school in New York City later in life. He wrote stories for children and, as I mentioned earlier, even provided guidance to a young James Baldwin—one of the most prolific writers of our time. He did so much in the short forty-two years he had. Looking back on his life, this final quote from his poem "The Loss of Love" really hits me hard:

The loss of love is a terrible thing;
They lie who say that death is worse.

I wept for Countee as I finished writing this chapter. He searched so hard for love in his life. Like his first marriage, his second marriage (to Ida Mae Roberson, a woman he'd known for a long time) left him unfulfilled in the romance he desired. But his inability to fully live in his truth also led to multiple relationships with men that failed. He seemed to be a tortured soul looking to be free. May he be the reminder of how talent and intellect can't protect you from a society unwilling to accept your full self. That you *must* accept yourself as you are and live for *you*.

JOSEPHINE BAKER

BORN: JUNE 3, 1906, ST. LOUIS, MISSOURI
DIED: APRIL 12, 1975, PARIS, FRANCE
ACTRESS, DANCER, SINGER, ACTIVIST

THE YEAR WAS 2006. Beyoncé was set to perform her song "Déjà Vu" at an event called Fashion Rocks. She was the opening act, and if you know anything about Beyoncé, you know she always changes it up for a live performance. The lights dropped and she came onstage thrusting her hips from side to side. As Beyoncé twisted and turned to the beat of the drum in a custom-made banana skirt, a woman's photograph was projected onto a screen behind her. The caption read "Josephine Baker."

Freda Josephine McDonald was born in St. Louis, Missouri, in 1906. Like many other Black folks in that era, Josephine was born into poverty. By the time she was eight years old, she was working as a live-in domestic servant for white families. And when she was only eleven, she watched white mobs (similar to what we know as the Ku Klux Klan) burn down several houses owned by Black people in East St. Louis. Big Nanny, my great-great-grandmother, had her own interaction with the Klan. They showed up at her house one day. But she was armed with a shotgun and was able to protect her family.

But Josephine had to watch her neighbors run from their homes across the East Bridge with nothing but what they could carry.

It was one of several incidents in which Black communities were burned down or stolen from us. Rosewood in Florida (1923). The Greenwood District in Tulsa, Oklahoma (1921). Seneca Village in New York City, a settlement owned by Black people until the city filed for what's called "eminent domain" and took it from the Black owners to create Central Park (1857). These, too, are parts of history that get hidden from you.

Josephine dropped out of school and, by thirteen, was living on the streets. She then met Willie Wells and was married to him for less than a year. Child marriage was legal then (and still is in some states). Think of Aaliyah's marriage to now-convicted rapist R. Kelly in 1994: She was fifteen. He was twenty-seven.

Josephine, at fifteen, was already on her second marriage. It was during that relationship with William Baker that she joined a street performance team—to her mother's disappointment. Her mother wanted her to work at home and serve her husband rather than be a performer. That was the norm. Hell, many still think it is. My grandmother Nanny would sometimes complain about this. How women are to be seen and not heard. Catering to their man. No identity of their own outside their marriage. The women she raised were always independent. My mom, my aunts. She taught them to raise hell if necessary.

Luckily, Josephine had big ideas for her life and eventually left her husband for a traveling performance group. Within a few short years, Josephine was divorced again, dancing in a chorus line on Broadway, and living in Harlem. All before the age of nineteen!

That same year, still just nineteen, she went to Paris and truly became an international star. Her erotic style of dancing (in attire that left her damn near naked) was a major hit over there. In Paris she debuted her most iconic costume—the banana skirt with pearls—

which influenced Beyoncé over eighty years later. It was also during these years that Josephine began singing.

Although her fame rose in France, she returned to Broadway in 1936 to star in the Ziegfeld Follies, but she wasn't successful. *Time* magazine called her a "Negro wench . . . whose dancing and singing might be topped anywhere outside of Paris." I would have had time for *Time* had they said some shit like that to me and mine. That kind of racism is why Josephine preferred to make her home overseas. Heartbroken, she returned to Paris and gave up her American citizenship in favor of becoming a citizen of France.

Josephine began her life anew as an expat. *Expatriation* is when a person chooses to live in another country that is not where they were born. Many Black Americans have done this before, from James Baldwin to Tina Turner, in order to avoid the racism and other painful aspects of living in the United States.

Now, hear me good. Racism is everywhere in this world, but it can look or feel different based on where you live. It wasn't that Josephine didn't experience racism in France. But in the United States, Jim Crow laws harshly oppressed Black folks. There were white-only clubs and spaces. White-only benches and fountains. White-only hospitals, which you'll hear more about shortly. There were "sundown" towns where Black folks couldn't be outside after dark for fear of being killed or lynched by white people. So yeah, Josephine Baker left the United States with no plans of returning.

And get this: Josephine was also a spy in the 1940s. When World War II started in 1939, she decided to work for the French. She would rub elbows with high-ranking German officers and other Axis officials during her tours throughout Europe and give any information she learned to the French resistance. She would also carry messages written in invisible ink on her sheet music between the

Allies, providing them with details about airfields and German locations in France. After the war, Josephine was awarded the Resistance Medal by the French Committee of National Liberation. She was truly a badass. A rebel.

Even through all this, she was still in search of love. She had four marriages throughout her life. While married to her fourth and final husband, Josephine had a baby who was unfortunately stillborn. This moment led her to making the decision to adopt, but not just one child. Throughout the 1950s and early '60s, Josephine Baker adopted twelve children in total—each from a different religion, ethnicity, or race. She referred to them as the "Rainbow Tribe." Other celebrities, like Angelina Jolie and Madonna, have adopted kids from various regions of the world, but Josephine was one of the first, if not *the* first, to believe in the vision of universalism.

She wanted her family to be a model for what the world could look like without racism and prejudice: folks from different places and religions being able to live with one another as brothers and sisters under one roof. All of her children lived with her at Château des Milandes in France, which Josephine turned into a major tourist attraction. She would charge the public money to take tours of the grounds to see how happy Josephine and her children were despite their stark differences.

Let's discuss the problematic nature of this entire concept. I get that Josephine was trying to show the world we can all be kumbaya. But that reality requires white folks wanting equality and being willing to give up power. Josephine wanted us all to have the same-size slice of pie, and eat it with the same utensils on a shared table. But that's not what this world has been about. White oppressors and colonizers wanted (and still want) non-whites, specifically Black folks, to make the pie, serve it to them, and have nothing for themselves but the scraps. You can't rainbow-tribe your way out of a white supremacist vision for the world.

My great-grandmother Lula Mae Evans had ten children by three different fathers. Her three youngest passed away in a fire, but she was able to save her other seven. I can't imagine her charging a fare to see them, though. And I get it, all my great-grandmother's children were Black. But still, it's not some kind of circus show to have a large family. By putting on tours of her family home, Josephine was turning her children into a commodity—mere objects—and dehumanizing them. Relating their diverse backgrounds to a rainbow reduced their identities to color alone.

To take it a step further, the terminology of *Rainbow Tribe* is also problematic. Growing up, I would hear people say, "I don't see color" or "It doesn't matter if you are Black, white, green, or blue." I promise you that everyone sees color and it informs how they interact with people. And I ain't never seen blue or green people.

Josephine Baker once said, "All my life, I have maintained that the people of the world can learn to live together in peace if they are not brought up in prejudice."

That is a very real truth. Children internalize what they are taught at home and in school, and such lessons inform their worldview in adulthood. If a child grows up with racist parents, they, too, are extremely likely to navigate the world with racist thoughts and actions, whether they realize it or not. If a child grows up around homophobia, they, too, are likely to navigate the world through a homophobic lens. That's just how it works most times. The important thing is what we do with those prejudices when we see them in ourselves. Are we willing to put in the work to refocus our worldviews for a more inclusive lens?

Josephine Baker's legacy is full of accolades: fighting for civil rights, being a spy for the Allies, and at one point becoming the most famous Black entertainer in the world. But she was still fighting her own personal identity struggles, too. Her own prejudices.

When her adopted son Jarry was in his teens, Josephine found out that he was gay. From that moment, she began treating him extremely poorly. Eventually, she was so upset and angry that she sent Jarry off to live with his adoptive father, her ex-husband Jo Bouillon, whom she had recently divorced.

How unfortunate it is that the peace Josephine was campaigning for was not afforded to her own child and other queer people. Sadder still, she never gave this peace to herself.

The truth of the matter is that Josephine Baker was bisexual. Despite having four different husbands, it was known that she also had multiple relationships with women.

Internalized homophobia is very real. People can be gay or lesbian or queer *and* homophobic. Look at the Harlem Renaissance. This period of great creativity, enlightenment, art, and queerness from the norm still denied many queer people the ability to own their iden-tity safely—either by societal constraints or self-denial. Many of the people in this book who were not open about their queerness had issues with other figures in this book being public about theirs. A lot of homophobia stems from a person's internal struggles with their identity. Because they are unwilling to accept their own truth, due to a fear of society or religion, they enact a violence against others who are queer.

I can imagine what that internal struggle could have been like for Josephine. Singer Tevin Campbell only recently told the world he was gay—after decades of shaming and assumptions made about him. Patti LaBelle confirmed that her best friend, Luther Vandross, was gay and lived his queer life in secret. Many artists and musicians fear the social stigma of being gay.

Fame doesn't always allow you to be who you are. Who you truly are. Josephine was a complex human. Who isn't? We get things right. We get things wrong. We sometimes don't get things at all. And it's okay to talk about people in their totality.

At an event in 2019, honoring the legacy of Josephine Baker, her son Jarry spoke about his mother candidly and without malice. Although he knows what she did to him was wrong, he told the crowd that night that he had forgiven her.

Josephine herself once said:

> *Surely the day will come when color means nothing more than the skin tone, when religion is seen uniquely as a way to speak one's soul, when birth places have the weight of a throw of the dice and all men are born free, when understanding breeds love and brotherhood.*

I can only hope that in the afterlife, she has found understanding and love for the queerness of her child. And even more, for the queerness of herself.

IN THIS ESSAY . . .

In this essay I will write

From my heart or from my head

                        How will I write

Evergreen, Investigative, Op-ed

                        What will I write

Does my opinion matter
Do they even care

                        Why will I write

Before I have breakfast
Before I sleep

                        When will I write

Should I even write this piece

                      Can you write it right?

Out of my mind and through my pen

                        Will I write

Through the night

                        I will write

RICHARD BRUCE NUGENT

BORN: JULY 2, 1906, WASHINGTON, D.C.
DIED: MAY 27, 1987, HOBOKEN, NEW JERSEY
WRITER, PAINTER

I FIRST LEARNED OF RICHARD BRUCE NUGENT when I was about thirty years old. I had been living in Washington, D.C., for a couple of years when a friend of mine, Guy Anthony, decided he wanted to start a nonprofit organization dedicated to uplifting and supporting Black gay men. Several of us came together to help him create Black, Gifted & Whole, whose mission is to financially support young Black gay men going into college.

To fund this operation, we had an awards show in Washington, D.C., that honored several Black gay men doing major advocacy work in our community. When it came time to name the awards, we wanted to choose people from history who helped shape the Black queer community. In doing our research, we stumbled upon Richard Bruce Nugent. We were blown away to learn about his work and contributions to the Black queer community. Before then, none of us had ever really known he existed.

As I struggled with my identity in childhood and young adulthood, I longed to know that there were people who existed before me. I was desperate for someone to look up to. That someone should have been Richard—an out Black gay man who was a writer and a creative pioneer during the Harlem Renaissance. Black queer kids deserve to know they have heroes. Richard ensured that his peers understood that Black queer people are just as important to culture, Blackness, and queerness as anyone else. Maybe even more important.

One thread running through the Harlem Renaissance—and this book—is an experience called "passing." In general, the verb *pass* means to identify yourself as something you are not. In the context of Black communities, passing occurs when a Black person with extremely fair skin (due to any number of reasons related to genetics) presents themselves or allows themselves to be perceived as a white person. During slavery, light-skinned children were frequently born to Black mothers who had been raped by white men. We can look at the children Thomas Jefferson had with Sally Hemings, an enslaved woman who worked on his estate, Monticello. As adults, two of Sally's children lived in the Black community while two passed into the white community. In my own family, there were stories of how my biracial great-grandmother, "Grampsie," could pass for white when she was a child and even at certain times as an adult. The word *passing* can also refer to the ability of a queer person to exist in heterosexual spaces without their queerness becoming known.

Because of his skin tone, Richard Bruce Nugent was able to live parts of his early life in a white community undetected. Richard worked as a white man in Washington, D.C., to earn higher wages and avoid the stigma of living as a Black man in America. That's a stigma that has unfortunately still not changed in this country, even today. He did, however, eventually become fully invested in the Black community throughout the rest of his adult life.

Richard met Langston Hughes while in D.C., and their friendship helped push Richard into a writing career. That is simply the magic that lives within Black folks. I always say you never know who will change the trajectory of your life. But when you meet that person, you just know—and you gotta lean into that relationship. It was 2013 when I met my best friend, Preston Mitchum. He was the first person to ever tell me to write (for a living). From that moment, I've never stopped writing.

Richard's friendship with Langston was also part of why Richard moved to New York City. This is one of several things Richard and I have in common. I moved from Washington, D.C., to New York to become a writer—but I was an out Black gay-identified man at the time. And upon his arrival in the city, Richard did a full 180 and began living his life as a Black gay man. He ditched his desk job to pursue the arts—another commonality he and I share.

I was a math whiz as a kid and young adult. Because I was good at math, I always assumed my career path would involve something with numbers. So I went to college and got a degree in finance. Even though I was great at math, I was also great at writing and orating. However, I was never pushed into either of those fields, nor did I know that they would become my passions. So, for nearly a decade, I worked in finance and did well. Until I lost the "like" for it. I'm not even sure if I ever really loved it.

It was then that I decided to switch fields and go into HIV work. I also started freelance writing. The writing made me happy, as did working in my community. The change in careers filled me with life. I was doing what I was passionate about instead of what I was good at. I loved how Richard did this, too, because I think more teens and young adults should follow their passions early in life. I made the switch around age thirty, but who knows where I would be if I had figured it out earlier.

What I love about Richard's writing is that it challenged everyone, even the greats within his own community. He didn't write like the other gay writers of his time. They—specifically Alain Locke— wrote about homosexuality much more covertly, using coded language and themes. But Richard wrote a short story titled "Smoke, Lilies and Jade" that explored an interracial bisexual love affair starring a Black man torn between a Black woman and a white Latin man. It shone a light onto a dynamic that existed in Harlem but that certainly wasn't meant to be talked about in public.

Alain chastised "Smoke, Lilies and Jade" for celebrating "effeminacy and decadence," a version of Black manhood he didn't think should be in the public eye. I found this to be very interesting. Yet again, it goes to show how deep-seated internalized homophobia and misogyny was during the Harlem Renaissance. So deep that even the heroes like Alain Locke couldn't make space for creatives who pushed against society's limits. Alain was essentially saying that homosexuality couldn't be discussed unless it was through a lens of masculinity and hardship.

It reminds me of our time now in the LGBTQIA+ community. You will often see a person saying "no femmes" in their dating app profiles. The community is still very anti-femme—because those who are femme are seen as a threat to masculinity. This is again a nod to the notion of queer people using "masculinity" as a form of passing in heterosexual communities. There is this unwarranted fear of gay people being viewed as femme. Even back in Richard Bruce Nugent's time, this was true. For me, it reduces us to our oppressors' constructs. I'm glad that so many queer folks, like Richard and me, have chosen not to live in those boxes. I hope we continue to free others still stuck in them.

I know that our writing isn't a monolith. But I can also understand the concern some have when writers cover certain topics that they deem harmful to the image of our community. In Alain's case, he thought Richard's writing made homosexuality appear weak. However, because we are not monolithic, we should be providing space for all our writings and perspectives. I'm grateful to know that Richard wasn't afraid to go against the grain with his art. It opened the door for me to do the same.

In 2021, "Smoke, Lilies and Jade" was turned into a short film by Deondray Gossfield and Quincy LeNear. I remember watching it and thinking how beautiful and poetic the story of this bisexual man stuck between two lovers was. It spoke volumes about the Harlem Renaissance, a time not only of heightened creativity but also of sexual exploration and fantasy—despite the societal pressure that forced some people to live one way in public and another in private.

Which is why it was interesting to find out that Richard Bruce Nugent eventually married a woman, Grace Marr. Their union lasted from 1952 until Grace's death by suicide in 1969. It was always unclear why they married, since it was confirmed they were never romantic partners. I'd suspect it was because queerness during the 1950s was becoming more scrutinized and therefore dangerous, especially for those who were public about it. So maybe the marriage served as protection for Richard.

Despite this, rumors swirled that Grace loved Richard and was intent on changing his sexuality. But rumors are just that. And despite Grace's attempt, Richard remained gay. In a 1983 interview with Thomas Wirth, editor of *Gay Rebel of the Harlem Renaissance*, a selection of his works, Richard said:

You see, I am a homosexual.

I have never been in what they call "the closet." It has never occurred to me it was anything to be ashamed of, and it never occurred to me that it was anybody's business but mine. You know that good old Negro song: "Ain't Nobody's Business What I Do"? And the times were very different then. Everybody did what they wanted to do. And who cared?

May more people read Richard Bruce Nugent's story and find the courage to live their life as unapologetically as he did. He is an inspiration for me and for future writers and artists who are afraid that their work can't push past the limitations of society. He is the reminder that change ain't overnight but is damn sure necessary.

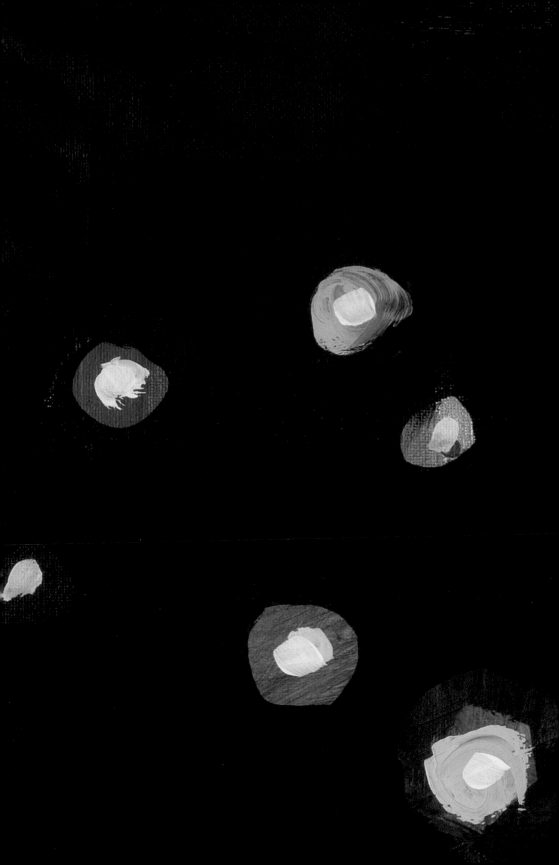

MA RAINEY

BORN: APRIL 26, 1886, COLUMBUS, GEORGIA
DIED: DECEMBER 22, 1939, COLUMBUS, GEORGIA
SINGER, PERFORMER

NOBODY DID IT LIKE MA RAINEY. She was the original trash-talking, take-no-shit Black woman. Now, her story is a bit of a precursor to that of Bessie Smith, whom you will hear about in this book as well. But as Ma Rainey used to tell it, she *invented* the music genre we know today as the blues.

The blues is a style of music developed in the Deep South that often used a storytelling component reflecting hardships and discrimination faced by African Americans in the United States. It also incorporated elements of spiritual hymns, work songs (like those sung by slaves laboring in the fields), hollers, and call-and-response.

Ma Rainey started out singing when she was very young, which isn't uncommon when you look at many of today's stars. You can easily go on YouTube and see old videos of Michael Jackson, Lauryn Hill, Jazmine Sullivan, and so many more, working on their craft from a very young age. Think no further than Beyoncé on *Star Search*.

Born Gertrude Pridgett, she was performing by the age of twelve in Black minstrel shows—which were a racist form of theater. White folks would paint their faces black and act out roles like Black folks were animals or otherwise not human. From time to time they would put Black actors in the shows, too. There were also Black minstrel groups that played out the same type of dim-witted performances to white audiences, but without the use of blackface. Back then, that might have been the only work a Black person could find. And that's where Ma Rainey got her start.

At eighteen, she married Will Rainey, known as "Pa Rainey." She decided from then on to take the stage name "Ma Rainey." (Think of Anna Mae Bullock becoming Tina Turner.) Ma and Pa formed their first group, called the Alabama Fun Makers Company, and began traveling and performing. Later they joined the Rabbit's Foot Company, which had a larger audience than their own group did.

Ma Rainey stated that her introduction to the blues occurred around 1902, when she was sixteen, although the sound didn't have a name yet. She claims she invented the term *the blues* after hearing a song about a man leaving a woman. She learned the lyrics and began singing it in her act. When asked what type of music she was singing, she said she called it "blues music." Whether this can be proven or not, it gives us a hint at the form's origins and Ma's character. This story makes me think of the many terms we use nowadays without ever really knowing who coined them.

Black communities have always repurposed language for specific needs. And the slang we create is often used—or appropriated—by dominant cultures. I hate the phrase *coming out* to describe the moment when a person publicly discloses they are not heterosexual. So what I say is that queer people are *inviting in*. I often get tagged or quoted as the person who said this phrase first, when in reality, my friend and former editor Darnell Moore actually coined the phrasing. His breakthrough allowed me to expand upon it. But those changed by the phrasing tend to be less concerned about its origins and more concerned about the person who allowed them the space to use it and feel seen. Luckily, we can trace this phrase because it was written down, but it can be hard to trace the origins of many terms, especially those passed orally but never recorded. Regardless, the words are in the world and can grow and change as people use them.

As blues grew as a genre, so did Ma Rainey's popularity. It was during this time she met Bessie Smith—another Black queer singer of the Harlem Renaissance. I love how everyone seemed to know each other during the Harlem Renaissance. Many famous figures were friends, and the rest respected each other, for the most part. The rumor was that Ma and Bessie possibly had a sexual relationship. Bessie also bailed Ma out of jail. One thing's for sure: Ma Rainey and Bessie Smith had a very close relationship.

The best one, though, is that Ma *kidnapped* Bessie Smith, forced her to join the Rabbit's Foot Company, and taught her how to sing the blues. This story was refuted by Bessie's sister-in-law, and I can't imagine Ma and Bessie would have had the lifelong friendship they did if this had really happened. Then again, that's the thing with rumors. There could be one side saying one thing, another saying the opposite, and then somewhere in the middle could be the actual truth.

In 1916, Ma divorced Pa Rainey and started a career of her own. From 1923 to about 1928, she recorded almost a hundred songs for Paramount Records, rivaling Bessie, who was at Columbia Records. Her recording career grew her fame far beyond the South. Ma became one of the most well-known performers of the Harlem Renaissance.

Her song "Prove It on Me Blues," recorded in 1928, has been studied by many. Angela Y. Davis, in her book *Blues Legacies and Black Feminism: Gertrude "Ma" Rainey, Bessie Smith, and Billie Holiday,* called the song a "cultural precursor to the lesbian cultural movement of the 1970s." (Maybe you've heard of Angela as an activist—a Black Panther wanted for a time by the FBI—and a distinguished academic.) The lyrics include these lines:

Went out last night with a crowd of my friends.
They must've been women, 'cause I don't like no men.

People say this song makes open references to lesbianism and bisexuality. Some claim Ma wrote it after she was caught performing sexual acts with several other women from her performance troupe at her home in 1925. An advertisement for the song showed Ma dressed in a three-piece suit, mingling with women while the police were nearby. It was clear that Ma Rainey enjoyed showing off the illegality of queerness.

I love how people who may not have been public about their sexuality during the Harlem Renaissance found ways to express it in essays, songs, poetry, and other arts. They were leaving us a road map for the future. With each generation, we see how what was once done in silence and in the dark has moved toward the light. We now have LGBTQIA+ actors, writers, singers, rappers, dancers, activists, and more, doing it all *publicly*. And every generation's efforts become a blueprint for the next generation to do even more.

Ma Rainey was also a bit of a fashion icon. Music intersects with fashion, especially when you think of the Supremes, Patti LaBelle, Grace Jones, and so on. But we rarely hear about that happening before the 1950s and '60s. Ma was known for wearing ostrich plumes, gold teeth, sequins, satin gowns, and gold chains. Her costumes were flashy, elaborate, and expensive. She was seen as one of the first musicians to introduce fashion to performance in this way.

In 2021, Viola Davis was nominated for an Oscar for her portrayal of the singer in *Ma Rainey's Black Bottom*, but not without controversy. Viola wore a fat suit for the role, which garnered a lot of pushback. People took issue with the portrayal of a fat, dark-skinned woman by an actress who wasn't fat. They explained that this was a form of oppression, since fat actresses rarely get roles in Hollywood. Much like we observe today with colorism and fatphobia, during the Harlem Renaissance thin, light-skinned performers often had stronger careers and greater acclaim than their counterparts who were darker, fatter, or both.

This is an intracommunal fight we've been having for a long time. Colorism, desirability, fatphobia, and homosexuality intersect for many people. One group with privilege oppressing another. It's why we have heterosexual actors portraying queer and trans characters. We've seen light-skinned characters portray dark-skinned characters.

We have a duty when retelling the stories of our past to tell them as accurately as possible. As many people stated with the portrayal of Ma Rainey, it would have been appropriate to use a fat Black actress. Her lived experience could have informed her portrayal of Ma Rainey and how Ma navigated society. We must hold ourselves to the standard of authenticity. And even when we fail, we should always invite criticism. I know critique has only made me a better person and writer.

The Harlem Renaissance has widely been taught from a local perspective, meaning that those who weren't living in Harlem have often been left out of the narrative. Nowadays, we have done a better job of linking people like Bessie Smith and Ma Rainey to the cultural scene. They had great influence on the period, despite being Southern performers. Ma Rainey may not have been based in Harlem, but she did perform there and had connections to many of its central figures.

That's the beauty of Blackness. It's expansive. It transcends our communities. Though Harlem was the epicenter, the Renaissance reached the South and Midwest, and vice versa. The musicians, artists, writers, and others all influenced one another. The period may be called the Harlem Renaissance, but it truly was a Black awakening across the country.

I feel like we are in a new Renaissance—and not just because of Beyoncé, but because Black queer people are shifting culture *and* being credited for that shift in a way that we haven't been before. Folks like Ma Rainey paved the way for us to do this from every corner of this country—and the world.

ALAIN LOCKE

BORN: SEPTEMBER 13, 1885, PHILADELPHIA, PENNSYLVANIA
DIED: JUNE 9, 1954, NEW YORK CITY
WRITER, EDUCATOR, PHILOSOPHER

I REMEMBER BEING A KID and learning about the Greek philosophers Aristotle and Plato. And as you know from reading this book, it was thought that W. E. B. Du Bois was one of our greatest American philosophers. In my research for *Flamboyants*, I found those three names referenced in an unpublished speech by Martin Luther King Jr. given in Mississippi in 1968. But the fourth name he mentioned, I had never heard before: That name was Alain Locke.

Did you know that Bayard Rustin, a Black gay man, was the architect for the March on Washington and Martin Luther King Jr.'s right-hand man? Alain and Bayard are further proof that Black queer people have been at the forefront of cultural shifts and creativity within the Black community — better yet, throughout the world — for generations. They refute the notion that queerness in Blackness is a new thing. Black queer people have been in the trenches from the very beginning.

Alain knew that he was gay, although he didn't really live in that truth publicly. I imagine this was once again due to sodomy laws and society's rejection of queerness, outside of its reflections in the arts of that time. It was almost like a don't-ask-don't-tell environment. Alain never married and never had children. But he did maintain relationships with many of the queer writers and artists he collaborated with.

Alain was actually born Arthur, and his ancestors were free Blacks. This information is really important, because slavery isn't taught with any nuance in schools. Many Blacks today are direct descendants of enslaved people who lived in the South. Before the Emancipation Proclamation and the Thirteenth Amendment, however, there were also some free Black people in the South as well as in the North. But to be clear, some enslaved people lived in the North as well. Popular history often makes it seem like the North was free and the South was enslaved. However, it wasn't that simple. Free Blacks existed among those who were enslaved in all states.

At sixteen, Arthur changed his name to Alain. I'm not sure why, but Alain also used to say his birth year was 1886 instead of 1885. Biographers haven't conclusively figured out why this occurred. However, this does remind me of the fact that my grandmother Nanny used to get teased by her sister because she had two birth certificates with a different date of birth. Suffice it to say, I'll never know why that happened, either.

Alain graduated with degrees in philosophy and English from Harvard University. He was the first African American to be accepted as a Rhodes Scholar. Here we go once again with Black queers being the first. However, that accomplishment was met with oppression: Because of racism, he was initially denied enrollment at Oxford University. Eventually, Hertford College took him on, and Alain continued his studies there in philosophy and Latin. In 1912, he began teaching as an assistant professor of English at Howard University, one of the historically Black colleges and universities (HBCUs). There he also joined Phi Beta Sigma, a Black fraternity. He finished his education at Harvard University in 1918, earning a PhD in philosophy.

After getting his doctorate, he worked at Howard University as the chair of the philosophy department. Alain had a passion for mentoring and teaching Black youth. It was something he felt Black communities needed if Black people were to ever gain equity in society. He once said:

> *The Younger Generation comes, bringing its gifts. They are the first fruits of the Negro Renaissance. Youth speaks, and the voice of the New Negro is heard.*

This relates back to the "talented tenth" principle I discussed earlier. However, Alain's philosophy was less about assimilating to white culture and more about self-empowerment. Which is why he eventually caused a major controversy at Howard.

Alain was let go in 1925 after fighting the administration for equal pay for Black professors. At the time, white professors were earning more money than their Black colleagues—at an HBCU. This sparked my interest as a two-time HBCU alum myself (Virginia Union University and Bowie State University). HBCUs were created because white people wouldn't allow Black students to attend their institutions, so we created our own. Although they are extremely important to the education of Black communities, many HBCUs still promoted assimilation, respectability politics, homophobia, misogyny, and more—mirroring the intellectual culture during the Harlem Renaissance.

I can't imagine being a Black professor—the first Black Rhodes Scholar with a PhD from Harvard—at an institution created for the betterment of Black people and not being paid equal to my white colleagues with fewer accolades or credentials. But that's the world we still live in today. However, I truly believe that things happen how they are supposed to happen. Because during his exit from Howard, Alain began working on a new project. In 1925, he served as guest editor for *Survey Graphic*, which called itself a "magazine of social interpretation." The March issue was a special edition titled "Harlem: Mecca of the New Negro."

Locke turned his work for *Survey Graphic* into a book titled *The New Negro: An Interpretation* later that year. This anthology included nonfiction essays, stories, and poetry by some of *THEE* greatest figures of the Harlem Renaissance. Pieces by Zora Neale Hurston, Countee Cullen, Langston Hughes, Claude McKay, and others were included in this now-famous text. Also notice how much queer influence Alain's book had.

I wish we were given the opportunity—especially as Black students—to read these types of books in school. As a Black teen, how do you know where you are going if you don't even know where your people have been? Our history lessons often went straight from American slavery to the civil rights movement. But do you see how much Black and queer history is missed if you skip the Harlem Renaissance?

We are too disconnected from our roots. I remember young Black folks in 2016 wearing T-shirts that said, "I am not my grandparents. I will use these hands," suggesting that folks would be willing to physically fight against white supremacy, unlike their pacifist grandparents. However, this assumption that older generations were pacifists is simply not true.

Many of our ancestors shed blood fighting for their lives and livelihoods, taking on great danger. Nat Turner led the nation's deadliest slave rebellion in 1831 and was hung to death and skinned afterward. Fannie Lou Hamer was beaten and arrested for fighting for civil rights after teaching a voter education workshop. And during the infamous "Bloody Sunday" on the Edmund Pettus Bridge, six hundred Black civil rights protesters were attacked violently by the police. *The New Negro* gives a lot of context to the post-slavery movement, and how we could build on our successes as a race without adjusting to white people's demands or assimilating into their culture, following their ideas on how we should live.

For Alain Locke, the "Old Negro" was the vessel for all the trauma and stigma and stereotypes of enslavement. The "New Negro" was the Black person who had self-awareness and self-respect. The New Negro's independence was a result of not only that self-awareness and self-respect but also the end of slavery and the start of the migration north. The New Negro represented renewal and rebirth—hence *Renaissance*—and the refusal to accept white people's bidding.

The Great Migration was central to my family's story, too. Our ancestors are primarily from Virginia and South Carolina. During the 1930s and '40s, a lot of my family began making routes north, primarily to New Jersey, where most of us are now. For Alain Locke, the migration represented the movement of Black people in all areas of life. It was our restart. It was the Negro of the South aligning with the Negro of the North, and the two creating a new world for Black folks.

When I read Alain's work now, it makes me yearn to read more Black writers of the past. To know what people felt and what they thought—whether you agree or disagree—often births new ideas. It also helps us take those things from the past, apply them to where we are today, and create a better future. I love how Alain understood that a lot of the work we do in the present is not about the generation we live in, but for future generations we may never know. It's why many of us writers do what we do. I write for our time, to help those here today. But the real work is done with the kid I'll never know a hundred years from now. And that person can use their work to help a kid one hundred years after that. Alain put it this way:

> *The younger generation is vibrant with a new psychology; the new spirit is awake in the masses . . . Each generation . . . will have its creed.*

A year after Alain was fired, Howard hired its first Black president, Mordecai Johnson. (Many HBCUs had white presidents and leadership. Some colleges were even founded by those white leaders, but that's another book for another day.) Mordecai reinstated Alain in 1928. Alain would teach there for the next twenty-five years, influencing generations long after his own. He continued to support and collaborate with other artists throughout the rest of his life.

Alain Locke is the key—pun intended. He was the key to success for many of his students, and the key to opening the world to the life of Black folks in a way we had never seen before.

BESSIE SMITH

BORN: APRIL 15, 1894 (POSSIBLY 1895), CHATTANOOGA, TENNESSEE
DIED: SEPTEMBER 26, 1937, CLARKSDALE, MISSISSIPPI
SINGER, ENTERTAINER

YOU EVER SEE THOSE PEOPLE who sing in the subways or on the street corner? Kids on trains with a boombox doing dance moves between stops? Or the viral videos of a regular person with a beautiful voice just singing their heart out? I've probably watched or listened to hundreds of them, maybe a thousand. And yet how often do we get to know their story?

Many buskers perform to make ends meet. Other folks just love to entertain and have never had a proper stage to do so. At the intersection of those motives is the story of Bessie Smith.

Bessie was one of seven children and lost both her parents early. She grew up in poverty, like many others from the Harlem Renaissance, so she became a street performer. Bessie was singing for survival, but she also had a passion for entertaining. It made her happy.

She began singing the blues on street corners in Chattanooga, Tennessee, with her brother Andrew playing the guitar. Eventually, her other brother, Clarence, got an offer to be in a traveling music group called the Stokes. But he couldn't take Bessie along, because she was only ten years old. He knew that someday his sister would be a star, so he returned to Chattanooga in 1912, when Bessie was eighteen, and got her an audition with the Stokes to be a singer.

But they hired her as a dancer instead, because they already had a star—Ma Rainey.

Yet it is said that Ma mentored Bessie and helped develop her stage persona. And so Bessie was ready to sing in her own shows within a year. At first, she didn't find much success. She was a blues singer, and the style was still finding its footing in the industry. However, by 1920, blues music was on the rise just as the Harlem Renaissance was beginning to boom. And Bessie was now becoming a voice to follow. In 1923, she recorded her first record under the Columbia Records label, the same Columbia Records that publishes Queen B—Beyoncé—today.

Not too long after, Bessie married a security guard named Jack Gee, just as her first record was being released. In the years that followed, Bessie became the nation's best-paid Black performer, with multiple hits under her belt. It is said that her rise caused some friction with Ma Rainey, yet they remained friends despite the rivalry. Unfortunately, white supremacy can force Black folks to feel like crabs in a barrel—meaning we are all fighting to be at the top. We pit ourselves against one another because we have been conditioned to accept the pyramid hierarchy of white supremacy as the structure for success—as if only one person can reach the top. That shit ain't never been true. There is room for us all. Nonetheless, Bessie was a star.

Although married to a man, Bessie was bisexual and wasn't afraid to act on it during her marriage. Jack was also having affairs with other women during that time. It's said that he loved the money but never the fame that came with Bessie's success. Plus, he couldn't adjust to her bisexuality. The notion of not understanding another's sexuality is riddled with heterosexual privilege. What is there for anyone to "understand"? If one can understand their own attraction to the opposite sex, how can they not understand a person's attractions to more than one sex or gender identity? Bessie finally called it quits with Jack following an affair he had with another singer. Bessie wasn't gonna be second to anyone, even if he was second to her.

Honestly, to me, the most impactful part about Bessie's life and career is how influential it was despite being short-lived. Between 1923 and 1931 she recorded about 160 songs for Columbia Records. She even had a seventy-two-foot-long railcar that took her to performances across the country.

Then the Great Depression hit. And without people's disposable income to buy records or attend shows, the music industry was one of the first to suffer. And just like that, it all went away. Blues music fell in popularity, and the money left with it. The industry was making a shift to what we now know as rhythm & blues (R&B) music, a much softer sound that relied less on bands and racial themes and more on electric instruments and background singers. Bessie, like several others during this era, was sliding closer and closer back to the poverty she had worked so hard to get out of.

Although she toured in the early 1930s, she was no longer the star she once was. As stated before, Black communities' issues with colorism and fatphobia are still very present in entertainment today. One could surmise that Bessie was seen as too "rough," too dark-skinned, and too fat by societal standards. She didn't fit the mold of the new era in music and arts—a problem that any performer today can also face. Conventional beauty, perceived desirability, and socially defined respectability win out over talent, passion, artistry, and truth.

Many stars were disposable during the Harlem Renaissance. Hell, we can look at our stars today and see the same type of exploitation. Groups like TLC sold millions of records but ended up broke because of a bad deal. Racism, anti-Blackness, and greed will always play a role in business and the arts. The greatest musicians of that time produced big hits, yet their royalties never made them finan-cially secure.

Some artists from the Harlem Renaissance overcame many great obstacles only to die poor and obscure. Yes, we're now giving them the flowers and recognition they deserved during their lives. But that recognition often leaves out their queerness.

Which is why writing this book is so necessary to me, and why you reading it is so powerful. *Flamboyants* can't convey these figures' full stories, but it is a starting point. You, the young readers and writ-ers of your generation, will be able to take lessons and inspiration from these lives and build on them in your own. Perhaps you'll even dive deeper and write your own biography of someone in this book, giving full humanity to their story.

Bessie's death is really sad to read about. In 1937, while on a narrow highway with her then lover, Richard Morgan, at the wheel and Bessie in the passenger seat, her car struck a truck that had been stopped on the side of the road and was pulling back onto the pavement. The truck's tailgate destroyed the roof of Bessie's car and severely wounded her arm, almost separating it from her body.

The first person on the scene was a surgeon named Hugh Smith. Seeing how badly injured Bessie was, he and a friend named Henry moved Bessie to the side of the road, where he bound her arm with a handkerchief. He sent Henry to a house up the road to call an ambu-lance. While waiting on the ambulance, they decided they would take her to the hospital themselves in Hugh's car. In that moment, though, another car came around the corner and hit his car, barely missing Bessie and Henry. Finally, two ambulances arrived, one from a Black hospital (called by Henry) and the other from a white hospital (called by the driver of the truck Bessie and Richard hit, although he never stopped to see if they were okay).

Back then, you had white hospitals and Black hospitals. There were laws that forbade a Black person to step foot in a white hospital, let alone a white ambulance. My grandmother Mildred always tells a story about how my father was said to be the first Black baby born at Williamsburg Hospital, in Williamsburg, Virginia. If I recall correctly, my grandmother's labor became an emergency and she had to go to the nearest hospital, which was a white hospital in Williamsburg. Luckily, they admitted her despite the segregation laws. But she was still separated into a different ward, away from white patients.

Bessie was taken to G. T. Thomas Afro-American Hospital. They amputated her arm, and she never regained consciousness before dying the next morning.

Following her death, there was a rumor that she died because a white-only hospital refused to admit her. That rumor was debunked by several people, who noted that no white driver in the Deep South would have ever allowed a Black passenger, so she never would have made it to a white hospital.

But that was the life of the Black American star. You could be at the top of the world in your own community and yet be disrespected and mistreated in the white community. Her funeral was held a week later in Philadelphia, with thousands of people coming to mourn her.

Pardon my tone, but her raggedy-ass ex-husband, Jack Gee, refused to allow her to have a tombstone, on two occasions even stealing the money raised for her grave. But in 1970, the iconic singer Janis Joplin and an old friend of Bessie's, Juanita Green, finally got one erected. Janis often told people she felt she was Bessie Smith reincarnated. They had similar sounds and were unapologetic about sexuality in their music. Another example of how far the influence of the Harlem Renaissance reaches.

Bessie Smith will always remain a pioneer for queer musicians and Black folks alike. She did so much in such a short time to change the landscape of music for so many future generations, for all of you. She was public about her sexuality and expressed that through her music. She was unwavering about who she was, and how her talent was to be respected regardless of her queerness. It's important that as we watch queer artists like Lil Nas X, Saucy Santana, Kehlani, and others rise, we recognize that their road to stardom was paved by queer folks like Bessie. And we can support them now, too, while giving Bessie her flowers.

WE GET LIT

Inspired by the poem "We Real Cool" by Gwendolyn Brooks

We get lit. We
talk shit. We

sing blues. We
drink booze. We

dance sin. We
are kin. We

are the rave.
Unmarked, our graves.

e's Terrific!

greatest sepia piano artist

Gladys
Bentley

MONA'S

UB 440
ROADWAY

GLADYS BENTLEY

BORN: AUGUST 12, 1907, PHILADELPHIA, PENNSYLVANIA
DIED: JANUARY 18, 1960, LOS ANGELES, CALIFORNIA
SINGER, MUSICIAN, ENTERTAINER

"**A** MOTHER ALWAYS KNOWS HER CHILD." I've heard this saying time and time again in my life, and for many of us it has felt more like fact than fable. But what happens when a mother refuses to accept her child for who they are? How does that child navigate the world, especially when their queerness shows up very early in life? What happens to the queer child who can't find love in society or at home? Those were life's questions for Gladys Bentley.

Gladys, the first of her mother's four children, was born to a poor family. But Gladys was immediately rejected by her mother—for not being born a boy.

She said in a 1952 interview for *Ebony* magazine, "When they told my mother she had given birth to a girl, she refused to touch me. She wouldn't even nurse me, and my grandmother had to raise me for six months on a bottle before they could persuade my mother to take care of her own baby."

By the time she started elementary school, Gladys knew she was different. She didn't want to wear girls' clothes, so she dressed in her younger brothers' suits and pants. She was entranced by her female teachers even though she couldn't name what those emotions meant for her.

Because she refused to conform to gender norms, her family eventually sent her to doctors to be "fixed." This "fixing" was what we'd call today conversion therapy—a pseudoscientific practice (meaning one *not* based in science) of trying to change someone's sexuality, gender identity, or gender expression to align with heterosexuality.

Some of the therapies of that time could be more psychosocial, like spiritual interventions, counseling, and social skills training. However, there are also horror stories about ice-pick lobotomies (operating on the brain with an ice pick through the eye socket), chemical castration using hormone treatments, and even electric shock to genital areas.

Not much is known about what specific "fixing" Gladys went through, but we do know that it didn't work. It never works; it only makes a person fear their identity, not change it. Conversion therapy, pretty much a junk science, has been deemed harmful, even dangerous, by the American Medical Association. Can a person choose to not act on their innate feelings toward the same sex or differing gender identities? Sure. But that does not equal a "cure."

At sixteen, Gladys left home for New York City. She became a piano player and singer. Then one day she saw a job opening for a male piano player at a speakeasy in Harlem known for being gay-friendly. Speakeasies were a style of nightclub that illegally sold alcohol during Prohibition. She decided to start dressing in men's clothing and performing in men's attire. She got that job, and her life took off. It was around that time she also became known for being a little risqué in her acts. She sang about sex and called out men using terms like *sissies* and *bulldaggers*—slurs people used at that time toward effeminate men and masculine women.

Once again, the interconnectedness of the Harlem Renaissance is made clear through an essay by Langston Hughes, "When the Negro

Was in Vogue." In it, Langston refers to Gladys as "a perfect piece of African sculpture, animated by her own rhythm."

I love that Gladys was unapologetic about not being defined by her perceived masculinity (which is how many described her appearance and performances). She remained true to her identity. In reality, the notions of masculinity and femininity are constructs that shouldn't even exist, as there is no way to truly measure them. Societies define what is masculine and feminine; it's not a science. For example, men in medieval Europe wore tights and it was not deemed effeminate, though today in many societies it might be. In the 1920s and '30s, many places thought it was too masculine for women to wear pants and saw it as a sign of rebellion. This can be true even today, but in most cultures pants are no longer a gendered garment.

Gladys wasn't trying to pass as a man. She was doing what she felt was natural to her. When we break out of the boxes heteronormativity places us in, we shine with creativity and diversity. That's the beauty I see in queerness. To be clear, even today we still have many issues in the LGBTQIA+ community around masculinity and femininity and who gets to perform them. Many people feel forced to tone down their masculine or feminine traits because they fear they will be judged, seen as undesirable, or physically threatened. But there are many who, in the face of this danger, still choose self over societal boxes. And Gladys was one of those pioneers.

At the same time, her career intersects in an interesting way with the denial of women's sexuality in music. When we look at women in rap, they are always condemned for being overly sexual, whereas men in rap have never faced the same critique. Gladys Bentley was raunchy. She imbued her songs with sex. In one of my favorite lyrics from "Boogie'n My Woogie" she sings, "Roses are red, violets are blue, if you take my man, I'll take yours, too."

I'm reminded of the song "I'll Take Your Man" by Salt-N-Pepa, and the updated version by the City Girls. It serves as a reminder of how connected we are to our past, and how what many deem new or inappropriate is just the evolution of a culture we have always owned.

Gladys was known for her stirring songs, her piano playing, and her "cross-dressing" masculine appeal. She performed at Harry Hansberry's Clam House early on in her career, using the stage name Barbara "Bobbie" Minton. She became so popular they changed the name of the club to Barbara's Exclusive Club. After becoming wealthy, Gladys purchased an expensive New York apartment and kept servants on staff. She also recorded several albums that appealed to white, Black, gay, and straight audiences across the country.

Her career only started to slow after the end of Prohibition, which caused the closing of many speakeasies—popular venues for her. Unfortunately, this affected many performers during that time, and made it hard for Gladys to find work.

Gladys had several lesbian relationships, and even had a civil wedding ceremony in the 1930s to a white woman. For most of her life she had a real hatred of men—stemming from the trauma of her mother wanting her to be a boy. And this is where my thoughts start to wander some. Was her performance of masculinity about being her true self? Or was she always chasing her mother's one dream? Chasing her mother's love.

After the height of her fame, Gladys began wearing dresses and removed the raunchy content from her act. She also began caring for her aging mother, as she felt a good daughter should. This significant change in behavior could be earning her mother's approval and/or the societal pressures against queerness. It could have also been caused by federal legislation that passed during this same time.

In 1953, President Dwight Eisenhower signed an executive order banning all homosexuals from working in the federal government. Sodomy laws also existed in all fifty states; these laws banned certain sexual acts, primarily between same-sex couples, but they could affect people of different sexes and married couples as well.

The Joseph McCarthy–era "witch hunts" in the late 1940s and through the 1950s—which essentially encouraged the public reporting of queer people, communists, or anyone deemed culturally subversive—led to many "out" homosexuals from the Harlem Renaissance going back into hiding or denying their homosexuality in public. During this era, homosexuality was classified as a psychiatric illness, and people could be imprisoned or forced into conversion therapies.

In an article she wrote for *Ebony* magazine titled "I Am a Woman Again," which many believe she fabricated for her own safety, Gladys wrote about being cured by female hormones to correct her homosexuality. At this time, Gladys married a man nearly sixteen years her junior. She continued to perform at small ballrooms in California until her death in 1960, but her career never returned to its earlier heights.

In that same *Ebony* article, she wrote, "For many years, I lived in a personal hell. Like a great number of lost souls, I inhabited that half-shadow no-man's-land which exists between the boundaries of the two sexes."

Religion and society can have a damning effect on queerness. In conservative contexts, not having boundaries for your gender or sex is the equivalent to hell on earth and even in the afterlife. Gladys Bentley was likely a hero to others who felt just like her. I wish the love she received from so many of her fans could trump that one love she chased in her mother. Her story still serves as the reminder of how great one can be when they choose to live their life as they are.

CLAUDE MCKAY

BORN: SEPTEMBER 15, 1889, CLARENDON PARISH, JAMAICA

DIED: MAY 22, 1948, CHICAGO, ILLINOIS

WRITER, POET

AS SOMEONE WHO LIVES at the intersection of Black and queer, I've been told that my Blackness comes before my queerness. As if those two things can be separated when I enter a space. As if we must walk around as pieces of ourselves rather than whole people. As if our queerness will be a threat to our Blackness and the Black community as a whole. Claude McKay faced the same dilemma.

He was a Jamaican-born writer and poet. Although he was bisexual, he never really lived that truth in the public eye. At six years old, he went to live with his older brother, Uriah, who was a teacher. Uriah helped Claude learn to love reading and writing. Claude was also mentored by the philosopher Walter Jekyll, who would eventually help Claude compose his first book of poetry in 1912, *Songs of Jamaica*. Claude left Jamaica for the United States that same year.

A few years after arriving in America, Claude read W. E. B. Du Bois's book *The Souls of Black Folk*, which greatly affected him. He also married his childhood sweetheart. The relationship ended quickly, and Claude left his wife and daughter.

He became involved in Black politics. Claude felt that the focus on respectability and elitism shown by the leaders of the NAACP and the Black nationalism movement weren't in the best interests of a Black revolution. At the end of the decade, he traveled to the United Kingdom, where he became involved in socialism, and then on to Russia and France.

Despite being abroad for some time, Claude still became a force within the Harlem Renaissance. His poetry took a radical view of race. He made it clear in his work that he hated racism. He also displayed his love of Jamaica throughout his writing. In his sonnet "If We Must Die," he challenges Black folks to have courage to fight against those who oppress them. I encourage you to read the full poem, but these lines say it all:

Like men we'll face the murderous, cowardly pack,
Pressed to the wall, dying, but fighting back!

Claude McKay was a truth-teller. He was fearless in his depictions of the totality of Harlem. As a kid, I thought of the Harlem Renaissance only as a glamourous time. The movie *Harlem Nights*, which starred Eddie Murphy and Della Reese, always made the Harlem Renaissance seem so fabulous to me. The characters were dressed in elegant suits and gorgeous dresses. The scene was about opulence. Even Michael Jackson's "Smooth Criminal" video made the Harlem Renaissance seem cool and stylish.

If we did study the Harlem Renaissance in school, it was only from this place of opulence and creativity. Harlem was the "birthplace of jazz music" and everything cool about Black culture. We never really learned about the lives of real people during that time. Black history is often taught in silos like this, where parts of the truth are left out of the narrative. Claude McKay filled in those parts of the story, even to the frustration of the most prominent figures during that time.

Claude's most well-known work, the novel *Home to Harlem*, was a huge success both here and in the Caribbean. In it, Claude painted a colorful picture of the Harlem Renaissance. He did a deep dive into the sex scene, the lower-income classes, and the less-than-fantastic parts. He talked about the nightlife of Harlem in full detail: petty crimes, lawlessness, prostitution. His stories showcased how many people during that period merely survived instead of thrived. It wasn't all glitz and glamour. Claude made sure the world knew that.

W. E. B. Du Bois wasn't pleased. He felt that Claude's "negative" depictions of Black folks were written for the white audiences who created the negative stereotypes Claude was critiquing to begin with. W.E.B. felt that artists should be showing only the affluent parts of our community, as a model for others to live by. However, Claude felt that W.E.B.'s approach was more like propaganda than art.

This reminds me of Black leaders like Al Sharpton and others who want to "bury the N-word." Meaning they want Black people to stop using it. They believe that because that word was, is, and may always be used as a slur toward us—and one of the most hateful words our ancestors heard—that our use of it is also negative. But for those of us who *do* use the shortened form (*n*gga*), it is a term of endearment.

That word has been used in my household from my earliest memories. When my uncle says, "You know you my n*gga," it is his way of saying, "I love you, support you, and will protect you." We all repurpose language for our own benefit. The N-word is the same way. But trust I get it. Especially the generation that lived through the civil rights era and heard the N-word used against them. But there were also folks in my family who lived during that time who still used the repurposed meaning of the word. And I think that's okay. It's okay to have some people who don't want to use it and some who do. We can have all parts of our community's story be told.

It's great that people want to talk about our achievements. Many did believe in W. E. B. Du Bois's "talented tenth" model. However, this model shouldn't mean that we don't get to discuss the other 90 percent, or not see their lives as central to our journey.

There are some horror stories about how queer people are treated in Jamaica. And I want to be clear that most places on this earth are homophobic, but Jamaica is one of the most notorious. I've been to Jamaica several times, and each time loved it more and more. But I have also been warned that the things I do in America may not fly in Jamaica. I need to be very careful when I travel there. My experience in Jamaica helped me understand Claude McKay so much more. He had a great love for his home country even if he couldn't fully be himself there.

When I wrote my young-adult memoir, *All Boys Aren't Blue*, I had no idea that it would expand the story of the Black queer American past my own country. But now it's been translated into French, Spanish, Portuguese, and Korean, with other languages to come. Claude McKay's work also has a universal appeal that transcends race, gender, sexuality, and nationality—he broke barriers that allowed me the space to tell my story.

Claude continued to write poetry for many years—almost as a diary for his experiences moving through the world as a Black man. He has become known as a prominent liberal thinker of the Harlem Renaissance. It takes a lot of courage to live a life like Claude's. Unafraid to go against whiteness as well as elites in his own community who wanted to hide parts of our existence.

Claude showed us writers how to tell the truth. And to be unafraid in that storytelling. As we live in an age where books about Blackness and queerness are being banned left and right, I think about how Claude McKay continued to write more stories even when being criticized. I take that with me.

If I must die, it won't be in silence.

JIMMIE DANIELS

BORN: 1907 (POSSIBLY 1908), LAREDO, TEXAS
DIED: JUNE 29, 1984, NEW YORK CITY
PERFORMER, ACTOR, BUSINESSMAN

IN LEARNING ABOUT JIMMIE DANIELS, I came to feel he led one of the most interesting lives of the Harlem Renaissance. A jack-of-all-trades, master of some. (I like to joke.) But trust, Jimmie mastered everything he touched.

Jimmie was an international cabaret singer and dancer who toured throughout Europe and the United States in his early life. Most would say his main claim to fame was the nightclub he ran in Harlem from 1939 to 1942. Many celebs of that time, both white and Black, came to the club, which he named after himself: Jimmie Daniels.

With the start of World War II, Jimmie had to close shop. He decided to enlist and, as a member of the military, performed for the troops. After the war, he continued to perform at various high-end clubs throughout the 1950s, '60s, and '70s for patrons white, Black, heterosexual, and queer. His final performance was at the Kool Jazz Festival at Carnegie Hall, a few days before his passing in 1984. As you can see, his career was long.

What I admire most about Jimmie's story is that there was no single moment or act that cemented his place in history. Jimmie wasn't the *first* to do anything. No records broken. Yet he lived a full life with career changes, travels, men, friends, family, and so on.

He was simply a talented human and performer. A lover of life and others.

For every celebrity we know of, there are people like Jimmie Daniels, everyday performers who just do the work and break down doors and pave ways. Their contributions are crucial, but rarely are they celebrated or thought of as exceptional. My grandmother Nanny was one such person. She was a nurse, a caterer, the founder of a nursery, and the head of many different organizations—she even helped raise twenty-four foster children for the state of New Jersey. All of these efforts contributed to others' lives. I'm still leaning on all the wisdoms and words she gave me. She will never go down in the history books for simply living a full life—but she will always be in *my* history books. I am who I am because of people like her, my parents, my great-grandmother Lula Mae, and my grandma Mildred. The list can go on.

Jimmie was a gay man and was public about it. As discussed earlier, that was rare in those days. He had two main relationships in his life: one with a white man named Philip Johnson, an architect; and another with Kenneth MacPherson, a filmmaker married to an English heiress. Although it was illegal for Black and white people to marry in the United States at that time—yes it was illegal back then!—interracial dating did occur occasionally.

Jimmie's interracial love life lies at the center of a racist incident that occurred when he performed at the Blue Whale Bar in the Pines, a community on Fire Island, New York. (For those who need a visual: Fire Island is a long, thin barrier island on the southern side of Long Island, with various neighborhoods that have a history of catering to the gay community.) He was living there at the time with his lover, a white man named Rex Madsen. Rex used to throw lavish parties at his home in the Pines. It seemed like there wouldn't be an issue for Jimmie in this community—until there was.

One night, they heard a noise outside. By the time Jimmie and Rex came out, there was a group of white men burning a cross in front of the house. As you probably know, a burning cross was a common symbol of hatred used to cause fear in Black folks, often placed by members of the Ku Klux Klan.

Fire Island is known as a safe space for gay men. In 2022, there was even a queer movie retelling of Jane Austen's *Pride and Prejudice* set there called *Fire Island*. But not everyone talks about the island's racist undertones.

I have literally never been to Fire Island because, even today, it is still riddled with the same racism that many of my ancestors dealt with. It remains a largely white space. I have many Black friends who have gone and still go and navigate the dangers of racism there. Some Black queer people have even formed advocacy groups in an attempt to shift the island's culture to be more inclusive. And I've heard it's "not as bad as it used to be." But what is not-as-bad racism?

That's the hardest part about being Black and queer: You are never just fighting one oppression. You are always forced to fight against something, even in spaces that are supposed to be safe for you. If you are in Black spaces, you can be condemned for your queerness. If you are in queer spaces that are predominantly white, you will likely be facing racism. And even when you are in Black queer spaces, if you are too fat, or too femme, or too dark, or too [insert quality here], you will face some form of harm. But despite these pressures, Jimmie Daniels lived openly as both Black and queer.

There are many people you may never meet but whose lives you will change in some tangible way because you choose to live yours as you do. As an author, I often get emails, comments, cards, and posts telling me how my work has healed people. How I was able to put into words what they have always wanted to say but didn't know how.

For every person who does reach out, I know there are likely ten more who didn't but still had that same experience. People like Jimmie make me think hard about that. Jimmie was a public figure whom many admired even if they never said it or acknowledged it. Jimmie paved the way for other nightclub owners and cabaret dancers even if he never knew it. There are always people who break barriers in the face of oppression. I think about Jimmie the same way I think about Pauli Murray, a non-binary Black person who boycotted buses years before Rosa Parks refused to give up her seat in 1955, sparking the Montgomery bus boycotts. Jimmie became the possibility model for closeted queer people. He was the alternative ending.

CAN YOU ANSWER ME THIS?

Hands sweat with anticipation,
Mic in palm, calm, keep calm
It's just a poem, a song, an interview

Will you let them enter your view?

What will the first question be?
Will I say the truth? Will I tell a lie?
With each question will I live, or die a little more inside

Will I hit the first note?
Will I get stage fright and choke?

Will I forget my lines?
The nerves eating me alive

I breathe in deep. Sip from the glass to my right
As the white host goes "Welcome, so and so to the show"
I smile. Laugh off the jitters, playing the part

Then it starts.

Only time will tell how this goes, parting lips, tongue untied
"My name is so and so and I . . .
I . . .
I . . ."

ETHEL WATERS

BORN: OCTOBER 31, 1896, CHESTER, PENNSYLVANIA
DIED: SEPTEMBER 1, 1977, CHATSWORTH, LOS ANGELES, CALIFORNIA
SINGER, ACTRESS

Symbolism is a threat to actual change—it's a chance for those
in power to say, "Look how far you have come" rather than
admitting, "Look how long we've stopped you from getting here."
—**George M. Johnson,** *All Boys Aren't Blue*

THE FIRST AFRICAN AMERICAN TO BE . . . Black people
are still becoming "firsts." It's the lens through which a lot of
Black history is taught in school. We are taught to be only as great
as our achievements, which often leaves out most of our story. Every
time I would see a "first" as a child, I'd get excited. I had a glass-half-
full mentality. I used to think, "Look how far we have come." Now
I say, "Look how long they kept us from achieving what we have
always deserved." That was the first thought that came to my mind
when learning about Ethel Waters.

I used to think of Ethel Waters only as a singer. Of course, she
was one of the greatest singers of the Harlem Renaissance, one of
the best vocalists of all time. She performed hits like "Dinah" and
the iconic "Stormy Weather"—although the rendition we hear the

most now was from Lena Horne and Etta James. That's all I knew of Ethel before researching this book.

But Ethel Waters was and is one of the most important figures for us. She broke down barriers and kicked in the doors unapologetically, despite her life starting from a place of trauma. Her mother was raped as a teen and gave birth to Ethel in 1896.

In the Black community, we talk a lot about how violence is a cyclical thing. That violence enacted upon the parent can influence the raising of their child. Although she played no role in her creation, Ethel described the hatred she received from her family as a living reminder of her mother's trauma. I can't even begin to imagine what Ethel faced.

However, Ethel surpassed the odds. On her seventeenth birthday she went to a costume party at the Philadelphia club Jack's Rathskeller, where she ended up singing a couple of songs. Ethel wowed the crowd. So much so that she was given a job at the Lincoln Theater in Baltimore. But she made only ten dollars a week from her performances, because her business managers robbed her of her tips.

From there she went on to vaudeville, like other Black singers of that time. She eventually joined the carnival circuit and toured the country before landing in Atlanta, where she would find herself working alongside Bessie Smith around 1916. Bessie, who was a force in her own right, complained that Ethel was singing blues songs, too. Despite this, Ethel would continue performing there before moving on to Harlem in 1919.

She recorded with Black Swan Records, becoming the highest-paid Black recording artist for a few years. In 1924, Paramount— yes that same Paramount you all know nowadays—bought out Black Swan. Ethel eventually left that deal and started recording for Columbia Records—yes, that same Columbia Records.

In 1925, she began performing at the Plantation Club in Harlem, followed by a stint on Broadway. She continued to bounce between theaters and nightclubs, and eventually began acting.

Very early in her career, Ethel did identify as bisexual, but never in a public space. This is important when we think about the trajectory of her life and her successes. Publicly, Ethel was married three times to heterosexual men, but she was also known to date women. This makes me think back to Countee Cullen's story. There was pressure for one's image to look a certain way. And to be clear, being bisexual means just that. You can be married to someone of the opposite sex who is heterosexual, and your identity can still be bisexual. However, some bisexual people choose never to show their full truth to the public for fear of retaliation. When you read a biography of Ethel, her bisexuality may be left out of all the things she accomplished.

At the core of Ethel's story is her list of "firsts." First Black woman to integrate Broadway's theater district. First Black American to star in her own television show. And the first Black woman to be nominated for a Primetime Emmy. Accomplishing any one of those things would be a hell of a career, let alone all three. But what did being the first really mean for Ethel Waters?

Breaking barriers in all those spaces didn't come without conflict or struggle. She was still Black and a woman, two identifiers that have always come with their own distinct oppression—even more so when you live at the intersection of the two. Success doesn't negate the pressures that come with it. You're sitting alone at the top of a mountain that no one ever gave you the equipment to climb.

In Ethel's list of accomplishments, the most interesting one for me is this: second Black woman to be nominated for an Academy Award. The nomination was for her role in the film *Pinky*.

Many of us in Black communities know about Hattie McDaniel being the first Black woman to be nominated for an Academy Award. But do we know the second person to do it? Therein lies the problem with symbolism. What happens after history is made? Do things change? Or is that symbolic moment simply used as the token, an excuse? The first gets remembered, but what about the tenth? When do we get to a point where there are so many Black people achieving historic success that the order in which they do it isn't even a thing anymore? That's my goal. To find my success and help others do the same.

I'm sure that I am a first of something or will be a first one day. But it doesn't matter to me if I ain't making sure that number eventually has some zeroes after it. Unfortunately, that's not everyone's mentality. I think gatekeeping occurs because we have seen so many "seconds" be forgotten. People who make it to the top will give you a rope to climb rather than stairs or the elevator. You know, the whole "I struggled, so you need to struggle, too" refrain.

Ethel once said:

> *The white audiences thought I was white, my features being what they are, and at every performance I'd have to take off my gloves to prove I was a spade.*

This quote raises a question: Were a lot of Ethel's "firsts" because people thought she was white? Was she a palatable Black woman to the white folks who dominated the decision-making process in show business? Even if it was, I love that Ethel never denied her Blackness and took it a step further to make sure those in the room knew it, too. She refused to be the token or the symbol of "change."

It speaks to the importance of showing up in rooms and being who you are. I've discussed the notion of showing up as pieces of our identity for safety reasons and convenience—both valid. However, there is power in showing up as your full self, in disallowing the powers that be to strip you of parts of your identity. Like the spade on a playing card, Ethel was a Black symbol surrounded by whiteness. She refused to let that spade be anything else.

ZORA NEALE HURSTON

BORN: JANUARY 7, 1891, NOTASULGA, ALABAMA
DIED: JANUARY 28, 1960, FORT PIERCE, FLORIDA
AUTHOR, ANTHROPOLOGIST

I WAS RECENTLY ASKED, "If someone were to write about you after you passed away, what would you want them to say?" My response is pretty simple: "I want them to tell the truth. The good, the bad. The in-between. I don't want to be on a pedestal. I don't want anyone fighting over the decisions I made in my life, debating if I deserve to be grieved." At the end of her life, Cicely Tyson said, "I did my best." I'm doing my best. And I'm closing this book with someone who, despite all she contributed to this world, had to wait decades for folks to say the things that she deserved to hear before she passed away.

Zora Neale Hurston died poor and was buried in an unmarked grave. I'm going to start there because out of everyone in this book, she is likely the most important, most influential, and most talented person of the Harlem Renaissance—and just maybe of the Black lexicon of thought. It's painful to learn time and time again how many of our greats died in poverty. I'm glad that who she is to us in her afterlife is much better than we treated her while she was alive.

I was a teenager when I first learned who Zora was. I remember it clear as day. Oprah Winfrey was presenting the TV original film *Their Eyes Were Watching God*, starring Halle Berry and based on Zora's book of the same name. The night it premiered, I sat in the living room watching it with my mother, as we often did when TV movies came out. The film received a lot of pushback because it didn't touch on the rawest parts of Zora's novel. But that's a common theme in Zora's legacy. Her hard truths were simply too much for people.

Zora said in her autobiography, *Dust Tracks on a Road*, "I wrote *Their Eyes Were Watching God* in Haiti. It was dammed up in me . . . I wish that I could write it again. In fact, I regret all of my books. It is one of the tragedies of life that one cannot have all the wisdom one is ever to possess in the beginning." She then went on to say, "If writers were too wise, perhaps no books would be written at all."

I know years from now I will come back to this book and think, "I should have said this" or "I shouldn't have said that." However, that's the beauty in writing. What I don't say now can be said in a new work years from now. What I get wrong here, I can get right elsewhere. But there is nothing to get right or wrong if I never sit down and take the time to dig deep into the pit of my soul to tell a story.

Although *Their Eyes Were Watching God* is Zora's most remembered work, her personal story is so much more.

Zora Neale Hurston was technically born in Notasulga, Alabama, but she never claimed it as her home. When asked throughout her life where she was from, she would say she was from Eatonville, Florida, the place she moved to as a young child. Zora truly embodied her Southern roots. From speaking with a drawl to the way her words and grammar were tied together, she saw the importance of language. And she understood that Black languages and accents were never monolithic—what many now call African American Vernacular English (AAVE) used to be seen as an unacceptable way to speak. Zora did not judge language as "proper" versus "improper," as some Black intellectuals of her time did.

People often tell me that I tend to write and text exactly how I talk. Meaning they always read things in my sassy, kinda-Southern-twang voice. They say Zora was like that, too.

Zora was thirteen when her mother passed away. Her father quickly remarried, and sent her off to boarding school. However, her father later stopped paying tuition, so she had to drop out. Zora had a real passion for education and refused to let setbacks hold her up. She worked odd jobs before finding herself in Baltimore, Maryland, where she began attending Morgan College, which we now know as the HBCU Morgan State University. In order to qualify for free tuition, Zora lied about her age, saying she was born in 1901 rather than 1891, making her sixteen years old when she was really twenty-six.

Thankfully, she was never caught. After graduating from high school, she went to Howard University in Washington, D.C., to earn an associate's degree. In 1925, she attended Barnard College and became the first Black American woman to graduate from the school. She was thirty-seven when she finally completed her education with a BA in anthropology in 1928.

Hurston was paid by Charlotte Osgood Mason, an American philanthropist, to travel the American South and record Black traditions, including folklore, literature, and hoodoo—a practice encompassing spiritual elements from various religions and indigenous ways of knowing, originally created by enslaved Africans in the United States. Essentially, Zora's work has become an important time capsule of Black histories that otherwise may have never been so thoroughly studied.

During the late 1920s and early '30s, she lived in Harlem, where she befriended Langston Hughes, Countee Cullen, Alain Locke, and Wallace Thurman. Together they considered themselves the

"Niggerati." They started a magazine called *FIRE!!* Although it only had one issue, it caused quite the controversy: It contained stories and images of homosexuality and even prostitution.

I think this is a great time to discuss the discord around Zora. Some speculate that she was bisexual. There is a reason I opened this book with Langston Hughes, a figure whose sexuality some still question, and close with Zora.

Zora was married three times in her life, each time to a man. Two of these relationships lasted for a few years, and the other only ten months. I couldn't find much information about her being in a lesbian relationship. However, one could view her writings about lesbianism, specifically in *Their Eyes Were Watching God*, as a window into who she was. Many of the Harlem Renaissance writers who never publicly identified as queer wrote about queerness, almost as if they lived vicariously through their works.

Zora once wrote:

> *If you are silent in your pain,*
> *they will kill you and say you enjoyed it.*

I've seen this quote hundreds of times. It has become one of the most well-known quotes in the Black community, a rallying cry for many of us afraid to speak up and speak out against the atrocities we face. There is a real fear of death when one fights against the oppressor. However, not speaking out about injustice has never thwarted death, but only delayed it.

As great as the Harlem Renaissance was, there was also a good deal of silencing. Interestingly enough, I've always thought of that quote from Zora and linked it to white supremacy. But in thinking of it now, I see that it also talks about the silencing we experience from our own. Even in spaces created by us, for us, many of us are not allowed to have a voice or be our full selves.

Zora and several other writers refused to be silent about the Black communities they represented—even if not fully discussing their queer identities in the public sphere.

Zora wasn't afraid to speak her mind, which is partly why she had such a hard life in the end. She even foretold her own fate in a letter to W. E. B. Du Bois, where she asked him to gather resources to ensure that notable Blacks would not be buried in unmarked graves and fade away from history. This was not done, and as this book has showcased, Bessie Smith and Zora Neale Hurston were both buried in unmarked graves.

Although celebrated as one of the greatest figures of the Harlem Renaissance early on, she lived the last decade of her life in decline— both in the public eye and in her own community. So when she died, there was no one there to herald her or ensure that her work would be preserved.

Zora Neale Hurston passed away in 1960, broke and alone in a county-run nursing home. Workers at the nursing home were directed to *burn* all of her manuscripts and belongings since she had neither kin nearby nor any children. A Black police officer named Patrick DuVal knew Hurston, and he knew about the plans to burn all her items. He got to the nursing home just as a barrel filled with her things began to smoke. He put out the fire and essentially saved one of the most important writing collections of our time. But Zora herself had effectively been forgotten.

That was until nearly fifteen years after her death, when Alice Walker—the author of the iconic novel *The Color Purple*—wrote an essay for *Ms.* magazine titled "In Search of Zora Neale Hurston." This essay prompted a resurgence in interest for all of her works. Publishers even began reprinting her stories.

Another quote from Zora:

All my skinfolk ain't kinfolk.

I think this quote sums up so many of the different -isms, -phobias, and -ogynys in this book. As much as we want to believe that Black folks are here for other Black folks, our communities still have so much healing and learning to do—including the *un*learning of colonialism.

Looking at the Harlem Renaissance, looking at how Zora was treated throughout her life, looking at how all of these figures had such obstacles to overcome from white folks and Black folks alike, it is easy to understand how Zora concluded that the people in her community would allow her legacy to be erased. That ain't family. That ain't kin.

I've seen so many say, "I was called the F-word before I was ever called the N-word." Although this may be true for them, it is too generalized. If you only live in Black communities, as I did growing up, it would be less likely for you to ever hear the N-word—used as a slur, not the way we use it as a term of endearment. However, because I existed around mainly Black people, the othering of my existence was wrapped up in my queerness—which is why the F-word was my first slur.

As glamourous as the Harlem Renaissance seemed, as culturally shifting as it was, it didn't stop the problems that continue to plague our community: Black folks opting to pass for white rather than existing in their own community—for reasons ranging from convenience to privilege to safety. Heterosexual Black folks being unaccepting of Black queer people. Black men criticizing and shaming the work and performance of Black women. Hierarchies based on class, gender, and identity—assimilating to the same oppressions we see throughout the white community.

Zora shouldn't have had to wait till the afterlife to feel the love that she now receives from her skinfolk. This book is a small contribution in the reclamation of these important figures, who deserve their legacy to be told in its totality. Figures who deserve the love of kinfolk *and* skinfolk. A love without conditions. A love that never requires them to show up as pieces of themselves in order to be acknowledged.

Zora may have been buried in an unmarked grave, but today we know her name and what she meant. Alice Walker gave Zora a headstone that states, "Zora Neale Hurston. A Genius of the South."

And that's how many of us remember her, as a genius. That's how we should honestly remember all the figures in this book. Some of the greatest geniuses we may have ever known. I call them "the Flamboyants." Their lives were full of color, wisdom, and experiences that shined brightly beyond the confines of their time.

FLAMBOYANTS

For too long, our true stories have been untold
Lies about us bought and sold
Ancestors to many we should have been
Muted were our lives, our queering deemed sin
But we dreamed, we danced, we sexed, we lived
On the tips of mountaintops we lived
The stage of the Great White Way we lived
Streets of Harlem we paved, we lived
Yet too long our stories have been untold
Ripped from history, stolen like gold
We live again, and now we thrive
Through stories told by the new negro, we thrive
From tongues of the youth our truth, we thrive
Flamboyantly our spirits remain,
A new generation's rage lit by our flame

RECOMMENDED READING

Here are some of the sources I used to learn more about the Flamboyants profiled in this book. I loved reading about them and hope you do, too!

African American Intellectual History Society (www.aaihs.org)

BlackPast (www.blackpast.org)

Encyclopedia of African American History

Harlem World Magazine

Library of Congress (www.loc.gov)

National Museum of African American History and Culture (nmaahc.si.edu)

New-York Historical Society (www.nyhistory.org)

Poetry.org (poetry.org)

PoetryFoundation.org (www.poetryfoundation.org)

Sankofa.org (sankofa.org)

Schomburg Center for Research in Black Culture (www.nypl.org/locations /schomburg)

The Legacy Project (legacyprojectchicago.org)

LANGSTON HUGHES

Hughes, Langston. "Let America Be America Again." Poets.org. poets.org /poem/let-america-be-america-again.

Hughes, Langston. "When the Negro Was in Vogue." 20th Cent. American Lit, alyssah20thcenturylit.weebly.com/when-the-negro-was-in-vogue-by -langston-hughes.html.

"Langston Hughes: The Poetic Inspiration for Lorraine Hansberry." A Noise Within, March 29, 2018. www.anoisewithin.org/langston-hughes-poetic -inspiration-lorraine-hansberry/.

See, Sam. "'Spectacles in Color': The Primitive Drag of Langston Hughes."
   PMLA 124, no. 3 (May 2009): 798–816. www.jstor.org/stable/25614324.

COUNTEE CULLEN

"Countee Cullen Branch, New York Public Library." NYC LGBT Historic Sites
Project.

www.nyclgbtsites.org/site/countee-cullen-branch-new-york-public-library/.

JOSEPHINE BAKER

Denéchère, Yves. "Josephine Baker's 'Rainbow Tribe' and the Pursuit
   of Universal Brotherhood." The Conversation, November 30, 2021.
   theconversation.com/amp/josephine-bakers-rainbow-tribe-and-the-pursuit
   -of-universal-brotherhood-172714.

Jackson, Lauren Michelle. "Josephine Baker Was the Star France Wanted—and
   the Spy It Needed." *The New Yorker*, August 8, 2022. www.newyorker.com
   /magazine/2022/08/15/josephine-baker-was-the-star-france-wanted-and
   -the-spy-it-needed-damien-lewis-agent-josephine.

"Josephine Baker: Tribute to a Great Lady." Château & Jardins des Milandes.
www.milandes.com/en/josephine-baker/.

RICHARD BRUCE NUGENT

"Richard Bruce Nugent Papers." Beinecke Rare Book & Manuscript Library,
beinecke.library.yale.edu/article/richard-bruce-nugent-papers-0.

Nugent, Richard Bruce. "Smoke, Lilies and Jade." *Fire!! A Quarterly Devoted to
   the Younger Negro Artists* 1, no. 1 (1926): 33–39. www.google.com/books
   /edition/Fire/-4sRAQAAMAAJ?hl=en&gbpv=1.

MA RAINEY

Brandman, Mariana. "Gertrude 'Ma' Rainey." National Women's History
   Museum, 2021. www.womenshistory.org/education-resources/biographies
   /gertrude-ma-rainey.

Chow, Andrew R. "Ma Rainey Is Best Known as a Pioneer of the Blues. But She
   Broke More Than Musical Barriers." *Time*, December 18, 2020. time.com
   /5923096/ma-rainey-true-story/.

Davis, Angela Y. *Blues Legacies and Black Feminism: Gertrude "Ma" Rainey, Bessie Smith, and Billie Holiday.* New York: Vintage, 1998.

Smith, David. "'All They Want Is My Voice': The Real Story of 'Mother of the Blues' Ma Rainey." *The Guardian,* December 15, 2020. www.theguardian.com /music/2020/dec/15/ma-rainey-black-bottom-netflix-mother-of-the -blues.

ALAIN LOCKE

Haslett, Tobi. "The Man Who Led the Harlem Renaissance—and His Hidden Hungers." *The New Yorker,* May 14, 2018. www.newyorker.com/magazine /2018/05/21/alain-locke-harlem-renaissance.

Locke, Alain. *The New Negro: An Interpretation.* New York: A. and C. Boni, 1925.

BESSIE SMITH

Day, Meagan. "Bulldykers and Lady Lovers: The Rumors About Lesbian Blues Singers Were All True." *Medium,* July 1, 2016. timeline.com/lesbian-blues -harlem-secret-f3da10ec2334.

Heuchan, Helen. "'Folks Say I'm Crooked': Celebrating Black Lesbian Blues Icons." *After Ellen,* February 19, 2021. afterellen.com/black-lesbian-blues -icons/.

Hughes, Langston. "When the Negro Was in Vogue." In *The Big Sea.* New York: Hill and Wang, 1940, 223–32.

Thompkins, Gwen. "Forebears: Bessie Smith, the Empress of the Blues." NPR Music, January 5, 2018. www.npr.org/2018/01/05/575422226/forebears -bessie-smith-the-empress-of-the-blues

GLADYS BENTLEY

Bentley, Gladys. "Boogie'n My Woogie" (1945). Genius. genius.com/Gladys -bentley-boogien-my-woogie-1945-lyrics.

Bentley, Gladys. "I Am a Woman Again." *Ebony.* August 1952.

"Gladys Bentley." Queer Cultural Center. queerculturalcenter.org/gladys -bentley/.

"Gladys Bentley: Gender-Bending Performer and Musician." *American Masters*, PBS, June 3, 2020. www.pbs.org/wnet/americanmasters/gladys-bentley-gender-bending-performer-and-musician-i0xlo0/14597/.

Shah, Haleema. "The Great Blues Singer Gladys Bentley Broke All the Rules." *Smithsonian*, March 14, 2019. www.smithsonianmag.com/smithsonian-institution/great-blues-singer-gladys-bentley-broke-rules-180971708/.

CLAUDE MCKAY

Du Bois, W. E. B. *The Souls of Black Folk*. Chicago: A. C. McClurg and Co., 1903.

McKay, Claude. *Home to Harlem*. New York: Harper & Bros., 1928.

McKay, Claude. "If We Must Die." Poetry Foundation. www.poetryfoundation.org/poems/44694/if-we-must-die.

McKay, Claude. *A Long Way from Home*. New York: L. Furman, 1937.

McKay, Claude. *Songs of Jamaica*. Kingston, Jamaica: Aston W. Gardner & Co., 1912.

JIMMIE DANIELS

"Jimmie Daniels." National Black Justice Coalition, June 28, 2017. beenhere.org/2017/06/28/jimmy-daniels/.

"Jimmie Daniels and Rex Madsen Residence." NYC LGBT Historic Sites Project. www.nyclgbtsites.org/site/jimmie-daniels-rex-madsen-residence/.

"The Origins of Fire Island's Tea Dance at the Blue Whale." Fire Island Pines Historical Preservation Society. www.pineshistory.org/the-archives/tag/Jimmie+Daniels.

ETHEL WATERS

"Ethel Waters." Bi.org. bi.org/en/famous/ethel-waters.

"Ethel Waters." *Broadway: The American Musical*, PBS. www.pbs.org/wnet/broadway/stars/ethel-waters/.

"Joy Out of Fire: Ethel Waters." New York Public Library, August 29, 2018. www.nypl.org/blog/2018/08/29/joy-out-fire-ethel-waters

ZORA NEALE HURSTON

Hurston, Zora Neale. *Their Eyes Were Watching God*. Philadelphia: J. B. Lippincott, 1937.

Hurston, Zora Neale. *Dust Tracks on a Road: An Autobiography* Philadelphia: J. B. Lippincott, 1942.

Walker, Alice. "In Search of Zora Neal Hurston," *Ms.*, March 1975, 74–89.

Walters, Tim. "Black History Month: Zora Neale Hurston Died Alone, Her Belongings Almost Burned. Now There Is a Festival in Her Name." *Florida Today*, February 25, 2020. www.palmbeachpost.com/story/news/2020/02 /25/black-history-month-zora-neale-hurston-died-alone-belongings -almost-burned-there-festival-her-name/1643050007/.